Purposeful Educator Connections

Deepen relationships with students, stay connected to your purpose, and improve classroom culture with this inspiring book.

Author Marcela Andrés offers five key principles to unlock connections with students, know your why, understand context beyond compliance, foster meaningful interactions, design high-quality learning environments, and partner with key stakeholders. For each principle, she provides high-leverage practices and strategies you can implement, a case study to crystalize the concept, and reflection questions to apply to your practice. The book ends with a reminder to put your own oxygen mask on first and a reminder of the power of human connection and the legacy you will create.

Now more than ever, we need educators to do what they do best and help shape the next generation of leaders who can change our future. This powerful book will remind you of your special ability to connect with students and have a direct impact on their life's outcomes.

Marcela Andrés serves as President and CEO of designEDengagement, PBC, a Latina-owned education consulting firm based in Texas on a mission to reimagine how educators, families, and community members partner to support the hopes and dreams of students. Previously, Marcela was a program director with a nonprofit whose mission is to advocate for public education. She was also a third- and fourth-grade teacher at a bilingual elementary school.

Also Available from Routledge Eye On Education
(www.routledge.com/k-12)

What Great Teachers Do Differently, 3rd Edition:
19 Things That Matter Most
Todd Whitaker

Passionate Learners, 3rd Edition:
How to Engage and Empower Your Students
Pernille Ripp

Your First Year, 2nd Edition:
How to Survive and Thrive as a New Teacher
Todd Whitaker, Katherine Whitaker, and Madeline Whitaker Good

Dear Teacher:
100 Days of Inspirational Quotes and Anecdotes
Brad Johnson and Hal Bowman

365 Quotes for Teachers:
Inspiration and Motivation for Every Day of the Year
Danny Steele

Safe, Seen, and Stretched in the Classroom:
The Remarkable Ways Teachers Shape Students' Lives
Julie Schmidt Hasson

Purposeful Educator Connections

Five Principles to Strengthen Relationships with Students

Marcela Andrés

Routledge
Taylor & Francis Group

NEW YORK AND LONDON

Designed cover image: © Getty Images

First published 2024
by Routledge
605 Third Avenue, New York, NY 10158

and by Routledge
4 Park Square, Milton Park, Abingdon, Oxon, OX14 4RN

Routledge is an imprint of the Taylor & Francis Group, an informa business

Library of Congress Cataloging-in-Publication Data
Names: Andrés, Marcela, author.
Title: Purposeful educator connections : five principles to strengthen
   relationships with students / Marcela Andrés.
Description: New York : Routledge, 2023. | Includes bibliographical
   references.
Identifiers: LCCN 2023033417 | ISBN 9781032510811 (hardback) |
   ISBN 9781032498164 (paperback) | ISBN 9781003401018 (ebook)
Subjects: LCSH: Teacher-student relationships. | Classroom
   environment.
Classification: LCC LB1033 .A525 2023 | DDC 371.102/3—dc23/
   eng/20230831
LC record available at https://lccn.loc.gov/2023033417

ISBN: 978-1-032-51081-1 (hbk)
ISBN: 978-1-032-49816-4 (pbk)
ISBN: 978-1-003-40101-8 (ebk)

DOI: 10.4324/9781003401018

Typeset in Palatino
by Apex CoVantage, LLC

Contents

Meet the Author

Marcela Andrés is an architect of dreams. One of her deepest beliefs is the power of partnership between families, educators, and communities to support students living out their life purposes. Marcela serves as President and CEO of designEDengagement, PBC, a Latina-owned education consulting firm based in Texas.

Before opening a consulting firm, Marcela served as a program director with a nonprofit whose mission is to advocate for public education. There she led the research, design, and implementation of an inaugural statewide family engagement principal fellowship for Texas. Marcela also served as the founding operations manager supporting the opening of four schools serving over 1,800 students and families. Marcela's career in education began in Torreon, Coahuila, Mexico, as a third- and fourth-grade teacher at a bilingual elementary school. Prior to her career in education, Marcela worked in the corporate insurance sector.

A native Spanish speaker and proud daughter of immigrants from Cuba and Mexico, Marcela is a world traveler, homeowner, business owner, dog mom, and graduate of Saint Edward's University with a bachelor's of business administration in finance and Harvard Graduate School of Education with a master's in education.

Dedication

To God, who has guided my steps and blessed me with purpose and inspiration. May His plans for me be fulfilled, for He knows the plans He has for me, plans to prosper me and not to harm me, and plans to give me hope and a future (Jeremiah 29:11).

To my family, my pillars of strength and love. Irving thank you for supporting and encouraging me to soar higher in pursuit of my dreams. To my loving parents, who have always nurtured my wings and modeled what leadership, tenacity, and humility mean. Your love and encouragement have been my guiding wind. To all my siblings, especially Alexandra and Moraima thank you for always cheering me on. Being your big sister is one of the greatest gifts!

To my extended family and friends, your constant encouragement and belief in my abilities have fueled my dreams. A special thank you to all my tías, especially Alejandrina Ceniceros (QEPD), Elueteria Thompson, and Amparo Ortiz for their unwavering advice and encouragement. Your selfless dedication to others has left a lasting impression on my heart. To all my dear friends, who I would need pages and pages to name and, more importantly, to thank for all of your support through calls, prayers, conversations, financial assistance, and words of encouragement. You have pushed me, uplifted me, and inspired me to be the best version of myself during my life journey. Thank you for doing life with me!

To the educators who invested in my life, I am eternally grateful for the investment of time and talent you made in my life and in the lives of others. Your passion and commitment to making a difference in the lives of children are truly inspiring. A special shout-out to Mrs. Tavasoli, who invested so much time and effort in our small family and community to make a generational difference.

To my community, thank you for embracing and inspiring me. Your stories, strength, triumphs, and struggles have fueled my desire to create deeper connections and make a positive impact for communities like ours. Especially to you, Graciela.

To Cynthia W., for the initial push to write something that makes my heart sing. Your belief in my voice and storytelling has been instrumental in bringing this book to life.

To my incredible editor Lauren Davis, thank you for your gentle pushes, insightful feedback, and unwavering commitment to excellence. Your guidance and expertise have shaped this book into its best form.

To my invaluable colleagues and network consultants in the field, thank you for your dedication, collaboration, and unwavering support throughout this journey. We are winning because of you!

A special shout-out to the amazing leaders I've met through network organizations like National Association for Family, School and Community Engagement (NAFSCE); Institute for Educational Leadership (IEL); Education Leaders of Color (EdLoC); Association of Latino Administrators and Superintendents (ALAS); Prospanica, Catalyst:Ed; 4.0; Latinos for Education; The Alumni Society; Latinas with Masters; and Goldman Sachs 10,000 Small Business.

To my dogs, Marcel and Zizou, who have shared their walk time with my writing time. Your presence and companionship have brought me joy and comfort in the midst of creative endeavors.

And lastly, to my younger self, who once resided in Apartment 101, thank you for persisting through challenges, doubts, and moments of uncertainty. Thank you for staying true to your vision and never giving up. Can you believe we wrote a book? We did this!

With love,
Marcela

Foreword

One of my favorite activities to do with my students is to have them reflect on their favorite teachers: Who were they? What did they teach? Why did they like their class or classes so much? How did those teachers make them feel? I have students draw these teachers, sketch images of how they looked. I also have them write words and phrases around these images that describe these teachers. As a result, words such as "enthusiastic," "too down," "made me feel special," "shared her snacks with me," "asked about my dog," "made me love math," and "was cool with my grandma," surround elaborate and colorful drawings of teachers. Most of my students want to be teachers themselves—I teach in the undergraduate education program at Chapman University in Orange, California. Following this reflection activity, we deconstruct what makes a "good" teacher—yes, having a deep understanding of the content is important, my students note, but a good teacher, an excellent teacher, the kind of teacher whose impact sticks with you years after you have taken their class, is one who makes their students feel loved, cared for. What stands out from these discussions is that my students aspire to be like the educators who made them feel special. These are educators who treat their students as human beings, as individuals who are more than just their grades and test scores, who show interest in students' passions, and who have strong relationships with students' families.

In the ever-evolving landscape of education, educators hold a powerful position—a position that goes beyond delivering curriculum and instilling knowledge. We, educators, have the ability not only to shape the minds of our students but to also empower them to become the best versions of themselves. However, we do not embark on this journey alone. Partnering with students' families and the wider community is paramount in unlocking deeper connections with our students. By fostering meaningful family-school partnerships, we create a seamless support system that nurtures students holistically. Collaboration with families and community members enriches our understanding of students' lives outside of school, enabling us to better support their growth and development. And this can be accomplished through the bonds we forge and the connections we nurture.

To become those transformative educators that my students aspire to be and to develop strong connections with students and their families, it is essential that we first pause and reflect on our own purpose, our "why." Knowing our why—our intrinsic motivation for teaching—is the foundation upon which we build our relationships with students and their families. Understanding our purpose not only fuels our passion but also sets the stage for authentic connections and relationships. When we are aligned with our why, our students and their families can sense our genuine care, dedication, and belief in their abilities. It becomes the driving force behind our teaching and other interactions with students, and our students can flourish under our guidance. Also, it helps nurture strong partnerships with students' families.

Our students and their families come from diverse backgrounds and bring with them a tapestry of experiences, challenges, and dreams. To truly understand and connect with our students, we need to step beyond the confines of standardized assessments and delve into their personal stories. What are our students passionate about? What brings them joy? What worries them? What are their families' dreams and aspirations for them? How can we embed these in our lesson plans and curriculum? By embracing their individual contexts, we can tailor our approaches, address their unique needs, and create inclusive environments where every student feels seen, heard, and valued. And most importantly, loved.

Fostering meaningful interactions lies at the heart of unlocking deeper connections with our students. It is through these genuine and purposeful exchanges that we cultivate trust, empathy, and mutual respect. By actively listening to our students' voices and that of their families, understanding their perspectives, and honoring their ideas, we create spaces that inspire curiosity and ignite a passion for learning. These interactions go beyond academic content; they nurture the whole student, fostering their socio-emotional well-being and helping them develop the skills necessary for success in life.

Designing high-quality learning experiences is another critical aspect of unlocking deeper connections. Education is not confined to textbooks and lectures; it is a dynamic and engaging process that should captivate and empower our students. When I ask my students to describe the teaching methods of their favorite teachers, they describe hands-on activities that pushed their critical thinking: from building roller-coaster models with foam pipes in physics class to cooking zucchini from the classroom garden in fourth grade to attending poetry readings hosted by the poets they read in their eleventh-grade English class. These are activities that extended beyond pen and paper. By creating these types of learning environments that stimulate critical thinking, creativity, and collaboration, we invite our students to take ownership of their education. Incorporating project-based learning, real-world applications, and interdisciplinary approaches, we cultivate curiosity and equip our students with the skills needed to navigate an ever-changing world. And it helps them see the connections between the classroom, their home and family lives, and their worlds. These are the types of lessons that stay with students.

As educators, we hold the incredible power and responsibility to forge deep connections with our students, uplift them, and partner with their families to guide them toward a brighter future. As I have learned from personal experience, from my scholarship and research on family-school partnerships, and from what my undergraduate students share in my classroom, relationships, human connections, are at the core of successful teaching and learning—and radical, empowering transformation. As I sit here, reflecting on how I can support my college students—our future teachers, counselors, school psychologists, principals, and other school leaders—become the life-changing educators they aspire to become, I am grateful for this book. I am grateful for its ability to describe and humanize such an important aspect of education and its potential to transform our educational system.

Stephany Cuevas, Ed.D.
Placentia, CA
June 2023

Assistant Professor of Education
Donna Ford Attallah College of Educational Studies,
Chapman University

Co-Author of *Everyone Wins: The Evidence for Family-School Partnership and Implication for Practice*

Author of *Apoyo Sacrificial, Sacrificial Support: How Undocumented Latinx Parents Get Their Children to College*

Preface

Mr. Spiky Slimy was fascinating to stare at.

My eyes kept wandering over to Mrs. Iris' desk where Mr. Spiky Slimy, the snail, was sitting inside his clear plastic cage with a dark green lid.

I was struggling to keep my focus and write the ten sentences for the prompt that Mrs. Iris had written on the green chalkboard: "Tell me about an animal you would like to have as a pet." Mrs. Iris noticed that I was off task and redirected me with a gentle smile and a silent hand motion to write.

In my seven years of life, the only pet I ever had was a small white rabbit that my father had given me when I was five, but my bunny had run away shortly after I received it. In my journal I wrote about a white bunny just like the one my father had given me. I didn't really even know you could have other animals as pets, especially one so small and peculiar as Mr. Spiky Slimy.

I wondered what his shell felt like and what would happen if I took him out of the cage. Would Mr. Spiky Slimy slither away or would he find his way back to his cage? I wondered if he would stick to the refrigerator at my house the same way he so easily stuck to the plastic walls of his cage. I wondered if he would enjoy ice cream instead of whatever yucky food seemed to be in his cage.

Fifteen minutes had passed by quickly, and Mrs. Iris asked us to bring up our notebooks and place them in the basket so she could read them later that day. I always looked forward to reading her short comments in my journal, as she always took the time to comment specifically on what I had written. I knew that she would be a little disappointed with me because this time I wrote simple sentences and that when I read her comments the next day, she would probably encourage me to write longer and better sentences. But I couldn't help it—Mr. Spiky Slimy was too cute and stole my attention during our journal time.

After our journal time, where Mrs. Iris would later skill-fully assess our writing and diligently evaluate our grammar, she had an exciting announcement to make. With a sparkle in her eyes and a big smile on her face, Mrs. Iris shared that we were welcoming a new member into our classroom family—Mr. Spiky Slimy, our very own classroom pet! Our classroom burst into applause and ruckus as she explained that each week, one lucky student would have the privilege of being the Classroom Pet Keeper, responsible for feeding and looking after Mr. Spiky Slimy's well-being. We were all very excited to have a new class-room role added and that this role would come with caring for a curious creature! As Mrs. Iris continued to speak, she mentioned that Mr. Spiky Slimy was an oxymoron, a term I hadn't fully grasped at the time.

To ensure fairness in sharing this delightful duty, Mrs. Iris devised a brilliant plan. She handed each of us a tiny slip of paper, tightly scrunched into a ball, and instructed us to draw a number. Excitement and suspense filled the air as I carefully unfolded my paper, and a pang of disappointment washed over me as I saw the number 15. I was one of the first students to draw my paper with a number, but when I opened the scrunched up tiny paper, my heart sank seeing the number 15. I didn't exactly know when the day would come that I would be the Classroom Pet Keeper, but 15 weeks seemed like FOREVER. During recess I started asking my classmates if I could please trade spots with them so that I could be the Classroom Pet Keeper sooner, but everyone seemed to be just as fascinated as I was with Mr. Spiky Slimy and nobody was willing to exchange their spot in line with me.

After asking several friends to trade spots with me and getting rejected, I decided that the only way I would be able to spend time with Mr. Spiky Slimy sooner was to take him home with me. The only problem was that I didn't have a cage.

That night when I got home, I looked everywhere for a cage, something small that would fit in my backpack so no one would notice. I was almost ready to give up on my plan to bring Mr. Spiky Slimy home the next day because I didn't have a cage, but then I remembered our strawberries were stored in a green crate that looked similar to his cage. Perfect!

The next day, during recess, I asked Mrs. Iris for permission to go to the restroom while everyone was distracted with games on the playground. Upon entering the building, I ran quickly to the classroom and took Mr. Spiky Slimy from his cage and placed him inside the green crate I had brought from home. The crate was small enough to fit in my backpack and still give Mr. Spiky Slimy enough room to move around until we got home. I left the green lid open from the classroom cage, and when everyone returned to the classroom, one of my classmates noticed the lid to the cage was open and that Mr. Spiky Slimy was gone. Our class looked around the classroom, but Mr. Spiky Slimy was nowhere to be seen.

That afternoon and the next day, I had so much fun observing Mr. Spiky Slimy at home. He did indeed stick to the refrigerator and the tub and even the closet doors. And he seemed to like ice cream, but I wasn't too sure since he didn't eat it all. His shell was hard but not spiky, so I was a bit confused about his name.

A few days later, I got really nervous when I read the journal prompt: "Is there ever a time or situation where it could be OK to tell a lie?" I started writing but again couldn't focus and kept looking at Mr. Spiky Slimy's cage. When I saw that Mrs. Iris was watching me, my face turned bright red and I tried to keep my face down as I focused really hard to write the 10 sentences requested.

While we were writing, another teacher came in and sat in our teacher's chair, and Mrs. Iris said to the class that she wanted to speak with everyone individually.

It was over. I knew I had been caught.

A million thoughts ran through my head, and I was afraid that Mrs. Iris would yell at me and tell me that I was a horrible person for taking Mr. Spiky Slimy. I was afraid that she would expose me in front of the entire class and tell them I was a thief and a horrible person. And I was also afraid that she would tell my mama that I had stolen from the classroom.

Instead, Mrs. Iris made this event a teachable moment I would never forget.

She went on to share with the class that she would be having a meeting with everyone to talk about how second grade was going and also take the opportunity to ask us if we had seen any-thing that could help her find Mr. Spiky Slimy. I wasn't surprised when she invited me to be the first one to meet with her; however, I did notice that she did it in a way of not making it a big deal in front of the other students. As we walked out of the classroom, I could feel the guilt of my decision weighing on me, and I was really remorseful for my decision. We started walking by the other classrooms, and I distractedly looked at the bulletin boards of the other teachers, mostly admiring all of the creativity that went up to showcase my fellow schoolmates work but primarily looking for a way to explain to Mrs. Iris what had happened to Mr. Spiky Slimy and what led me to make this terrible decision.

As we walked down the halls, Mrs. Iris talked to me like a friend with a voice that was calm and respectful. She started asking me general questions like how I was enjoying second grade and what books I liked the most. She commented on my high Accelerated Reader points and celebrated with me that again I would win the coupon for free pizza. I smiled half-heartedly even though winning the pizza coupon always made me smile. As our conversation continued, she told me how she has seen how much my writing has improved through my reading and had really enjoyed reading about my white pet rabbit that my dad had given me. I gave her another weak smile, but this time, I started to tear up. My father had left just a couple of years ago and that was one of the last gifts he had given me before he left our family. She noticed my watery eyes and asked me if I was okay. I told her that I was but that remembering my bunny made me sad because it reminded me of my father.

We stopped walking, and she crouched down to be at eye level with me and asked me if I wanted to talk about my father. I started crying. I didn't have words to describe how I was feeling, and I felt ashamed to share with her the details of my father's departure since I truly didn't even understand them myself.

Mrs. Iris gave me a gentle hug and said that everything was going to be okay. She shared that sometimes in life, adults make decisions that children can't change and that the best thing we could do was not try to take ownership of the decisions or choices adults make. Mrs. Iris started telling me that from a very young age, we all start making choices in life, like what to wear or not to wear to school or whether to do or not to do our chores and that the way we start making choices at a young age will create a pattern of how we make decisions as adults. Her words made me feel comforted and safe, and I felt very grateful that I had such a caring teacher.

Then she paused and reminded me that she was taking all the students out of class, one at a time, not only to ask them about how second grade was going but also to ask about our classroom pet. Since Mr. Spiky Slimy went missing the day before, she said she wanted to take advantage of the time and ask each student if we had seen anything that would help us find Mr. Spiky Slimy. She said she was excited to start with me because I was a great student that always worked hard and took care of our class-room. She also subtly mentioned that I was the only person to go to the restroom the day our class pet escaped and that she was hoping I had seen something so that I could help her find Mr. Spiky Slimy. I looked down at the floor and lied and said that I hadn't seen anything. She offered me a kind smile and told me that if I remembered anything at all, to please come tell her. Mrs. Iris didn't call me out, but something inside me told me that she knew I had taken him, but nothing in her facial expression, voice, or actions confirmed my suspicion. In fact, during the day, I saw her take other students out of the class as she said she would, and I assumed that she was asking them the same questions.

By lunch time, I couldn't take it anymore. I felt remorse about my choice to take our classroom pet home and was sad that I had lied to my teacher about not seeing Mr. Spiky Slimy. All my classmates were talking about how sad they were that Mr. Spiky Slimy was gone, and some were concerned that something bad had happened to him. It made me sad that my classmates were also being affected by choices, and I didn't want to make bad choices as a kid or an adult, so I resolved that I needed to confess to Mrs. Iris.

I will never forget how Mrs. Iris made me feel when I confessed to her that I stole Mr. Spiky Slimy. With the most compassionate eyes and tone of voice, Mrs. Iris thanked me for sharing what had happened to Mr. Spiky Slimy. With her gentle response and choice of words, she made me feel loved and cared for deeply and she taught me lessons beyond the second-grade curriculum. She acknowledged that my choice to steal Mr. Spiky Slimy was not a good one but made it clear that it didn't make me a bad person. Mrs. Iris worked with me so that I could share with both the class and my mom the choice that I had made and how to offer an apology. When I returned Mr. Spiky Slimy to our classroom and asked my classmates for forgiveness, everyone was so graceful and forgiving, and by recess, my actions to take Mr. Spiky Slimy had been forgotten.

What I received that day from Mrs. Iris was a profound example on how to be an amazing educator. And throughout my academic journey, I would learn many more lessons on what makes an amazing educator. Educators like Mrs. Iris who meaningfully connect with their students in the classroom have a profound impact on the lives of their students. And just as small as Mr. Spiky Slimy, educators can have tremendous impact through the everyday small moments.

When educators take time to connect on a deeper level with students every day and see them as a whole child despite their circumstances, educate them with the dignity and respect every learner deserves, inspire them to reach their fullest potential, and partner with the people that love them, education in the purest form takes place.

Unlocking the Contents: A Comprehensive Overview and Scope

Growing up, I lived in an apartment next to two commercial trash cans, and when I was enrolled in school, I was marked with deficit labels that included "at-risk," "low-income," "economically disadvantaged," "English-language learner," "single-parent household," and "minority." Yet, because of educators like Mrs. Iris and others that you will read about in the book, I am a first-generation college graduate with a bachelor's degree in business administration from Saint Edward's University and a master's degree from the Harvard Graduate School of Education and now a first-generation CEO of a national consulting firm. My story is one that went from poverty to prosperity because educators deeply connected with me.

This book is written to inspire, motivate, and educate about the very important role educators play in the lives of students, in their families, and in our communities. And while I know many educators grasp the potential of their impact, our society has done a terrible job of affirming and honoring the role of an educator. At a time when educators are fleeing this very important profession, my hope and, dare I say, gift back to educators is that as you read the words on these pages and find an ounce of inspiration and five strategies that have proven to be true in my life, you embrace them in your practice to further your impact on the lives of your students and your personal legacy. Our education system is flawed, inequitable, and, in many ways, broken, but I firmly believe, through my lived experience that despite this dismal reality, educators can exercise their personal and collective leadership to drive transformational change to ensure that my outlier story, while a great story, is the norm for every child, in every classroom, in every zip code. Educators connected with me in a way that oriented me toward truly believing in a better and brighter future, despite my difficult reality. They partnered with my family and community, and I can wholeheartedly say that educators are, without a doubt, one of the key reasons that all my dreams came true—and are still coming true.

This book is about five simple yet profound principles and practices to unlock a deeper connection with students and improve your classroom culture. The principles draw from my own personal qualitative phenomenological research (i.e. this is my story and the stories I hear from students and educators today). Additionally, as a former educator, administrator, and now consultant, I will occasionally embed frameworks, theories, and research by brilliant minds to further lift up the principles that my lived experience has proven to be true.

In the "Introduction: The Special Position of an Educator," I ground the chapter in the special position an educator holds in the life of students by lifting up the ecological system theory founded by psychologist Urie Bronfenbrenner. In "Chapter 1—Principle

1: Know Your Why," I kick off the first of the five principles and explain the impact to an educator's practice when they know their why and use it in the classroom to meaningfully connect with students. Additionally, in this chapter, I highlight resources from author Simon Sinek and comedian Michael Jr. behind the reasons leading with your why is so impactful. In "Chapter 2—Principle 2: Understand Context Beyond Compliance," I share stories about educators who connected with me beyond the labels placed on me and the impact it had on both my academic and social emotional development. This chapter explains the importance of understanding one's own biases, both implicit and explicit, as well as gives educators practical tools on how to communicate through asset-based and culturally relevant language that treats and honors students with dignity and respect. "Chapter 3—Principle 3: Foster Meaningful Interactions" is grounded in stories about how meaningful interactions with educators could have been the difference in my trajectory when I moved to an entirely different community that wasn't representative of my cultural identity or socioeconomic background. It showcases how the opportunity to deeply connect with students and foster meaningful interactions still exists today. Next, in "Chapter 4—Principle 4: Design High-Quality Educational Learning Environments," I will share stories about how a couple of teachers cultivated the love and joy of learning by ensuring they were delivering a high-quality educational experience in their classroom. Further, this chapter will focus on sharing techniques and strategies with teachers to implement in their practice and support them with curating memorable and joyous learning experiences. In "Chapter 5—Principle 5: Partner With Key Stakeholders," I introduce the final principle. Here I will talk about the magic that takes place when all the people who love and support students work together to support students' wildest dreams. This chapter will discuss some of the opportunities that we have today, especially after facing both a global and racial discrimination pandemic to work together in service of supporting students to reach their highest potential. Then, in "Chapter 6: Oxygen Masks Are Not Just for Airplanes," I remind educators that caring for yourself is so important when you are working to prepare the next generation and the need to ensure your oxygen mask is on before you support others is critical. The work educators lead is extremely important, and your personal cup needs to be full; otherwise, the principles in the book won't matter. Finally, in "Chapter 7: The Power of Human Connections," I end the book with two stories that showcase the power of human connection and how educators support students with their own personal legacy and that of their families.

It is my deepest hope that this book will inspire you and that my stories bring to life the special role an educator plays in the life of a student. As a gift back to you, I have some homework. And I promise I am not salty from ALL of the homework teachers once gave me! After each chapter you will have a short summary of the chapter, including five high-leverage activities you can use in your classroom with reflection questions to apply to your practice and journey of creating deeper connections with students. And because my educators taught me well, I've also included a case study, written like a *novela* (soap opera), to really help crystalize each of the five principles. My homework for you after every chapter will not be graded, unless you want me to, so assume that every time you finish your homework, you get a gold star.

Now, more than ever, we need educators to do what they do best and help shape the next generation of leaders who can and will change our future. It is an honor and privilege to have the space, time, and support to capture my thoughts, ideas, and hopes on the pages contained herein and I will not take this opportunity lightly. You will receive my full, real, authentic spicy self in every word. Grab a *cafecito* or your favorite tea because just like meeting with a friend at a great coffee shop and keeping it real—you and I are going to go heart to heart as I share the lessons I have proven to be true.

Let's get connected!!

Creating Space for Reflection: The Profound Impact of Educators

Before delving into the transformative content of this book, I invite you to reflect on the significant influence an educator has had on your life. Take a moment to consider the ways in which an educator shaped your journey. If you didn't have such an experience, envision the impact you would have desired from an inspiring and supportive educator.

By engaging in this reflective exercise, educators can gain deeper insights into their own lives and experiences with educators, enabling them to apply these lessons to their own teaching practices. It serves as a powerful reminder of the influential role educators play in shaping the lives of their students and encourages them to make a positive and lasting impact on their own students.

Reflection Questions for Preface

1. How did an educator inspire and motivate you to learn and grow?
2. How did your educators show care, empathy, and understanding toward any challenges and emotions you experienced as a child?
3. How did an educator serve as a mentor, role model, or source of inspiration in your life?
4. How did an educator partner with your family in meaningful ways to support your academic and social and emotional development?

Introduction: The Special Position of an Educator

Building strong relationships helps shift the mindset on how you approach even your most challenging situations from reactive to proactive. "Learning" your students, especially those who may lack many social and emotional skill sets, has everything to do with dialing back to the most foundational factors for us as human beings—who are they? How do they best succeed? What makes them feel safe, seen, loved, and heard? We are simply larger versions of the younger beings that they are. Maintaining an understanding that we all have triggers, limits, and needs helps to approach situations both good and challenging with genuine care and an empathetic approach to meeting the needs of students while simultaneously creating a safe space not only for them but for ourselves.

Nadia Abdalah, PK–4 teacher, Texas

Educators hold a special position in the lives of children, much like families. Their close proximity and deep connections foster a nurturing environment for growth and learning. Teachers not only impart knowledge but also provide guidance, support, and inspiration, shaping the trajectory of a student's life. Educators form deep connections with their students, understanding their strengths, weaknesses, and unique qualities. In the special position they hold, they have the opportunity to foster an environment where children can flourish and reach their fullest potential.

The story you read about in the Preface with Mr. Spiky Slimy and Mrs. Iris is just one of the googol of stories that exemplifies how educators play a critical role in a student's academic and socio-emotional development. When I stole Mr. Spiky Slimy, my interaction with Mrs. Iris went beyond her teaching me learning objectives from the second grade curriculum, helping to improve

DOI: 10.4324/9781003401018-1

my writing and grammar, but also played a role in my personal development. Mrs. Iris helped me develop the skills I needed to communicate to my mom that I had chosen to make a bad decision. Together my mom and Mrs. Iris worked to identify resources to support me during that season of my life. I don't exactly remember the name of the resources, but I do recall that I read several books and listened to audio tapes about the importance of honesty. Mrs. Iris understood the special place she held in my life and gently guided me to learn life lessons beyond grammar.

The rest of the book will focus on stories where I uplift the impact educators had on my life, but for this foundational chapter, I humbly ask to sit next to you as a fellow educator and share with you my experience in the classroom to further lift up this idea of the special position of an educator.

Before embarking on my journey in education, I had a career in the insurance industry, where I dealt with selling and under-writing various risks. Interestingly, as I reflect on my experiences, I often find myself drawing a parallel between educators and underwriters. Educators, like underwriters, play a crucial role in securing the future of our country. Through their dedication and hard work, they ensure that citizens do not fall victim to the perils that an uneducated population may face. Growing up as the daughter of immigrants, I have had the privilege of witnessing the profound impact education has on lives and opportunities. The transformative power of education is something I hold close to my heart.

A few years into my insurance career, I made a decision to take a personal sabbatical for family reasons and moved to my mother's home country, Mexico. Originally, I had anticipated staying there for a relatively short period of three years. Given the limited timeframe, I chose not to pursue the rigorous licensing process required to continue working as an underwriter in that particular field. However, I was determined to make the most of my time and channel my abilities toward personal growth and expanding my knowledge.

In my search for opportunities to grow my mind, I came across a private bilingual school that had posted a job opportunity for an English tutor. Perfect, I thought! I read, speak, and write English, so investing my time as an English tutor would be a great use of my days. But shortly after I was hired as a tutor, a fifth-grade teacher abruptly left in the middle of the year leaving the school short-staffed. (I know what you are thinking—that never happens in the US. Kidding!) The administrator approached me and asked if I would be interested in covering the class until they found a replacement. It seemed easy enough. I had been a student before. I had a degree in business administration. How difficult could it be to teach a room full of fifth graders?

Oh, how naive I was.

An entire day of taking over the fifth grade class hadn't even passed when I realized just how incredibly difficult it is to stand in front of students and teach, let alone educate them. From the macro goal of commanding the attention of the room to creating a space of shared learning and exchange of critical consciousness and dialogue, there were significant challenges that I was terribly unprepared and untrained to handle. Thankfully, because the administration knew that I lacked training and an education background, they were gracious and understanding with my approach to teaching. Weeks had passed by, and the school was unable to fill the fifth-grade teacher position, and thus, I became the permanent replacement for the remainder of the year. To this day, I am not sure if the students just liked my quirky jokes and advocated for me to remain a teacher or if the administration had only walked in to observe me on my "good days," but I wasn't fired, and when the time came for staffing for the next school year, I was also extended an offer to become a third- and fourth-grade teacher.

My first full year as a third- and fourth-grade teacher transformed the trajectory of my life. In my first official year of teaching, I learned a lot about myself, educating children, working with families, collaborating with other teachers, the role of school administrators, school safety, and so much more.

All of my students were Mexican but came from a variety of socioeconomic backgrounds and familial makeup. As an educator in a developing country, I learned that every student, when offered an equitable educational experience, can learn and develop critical thinking, regardless of color, economic strata, or familial makeup. It wasn't the labels that would determine if the students in my classroom would learn or the zip codes that they came from; it was my instruction and support, or lack thereof, that I provided that would determine if a student would learn. Now, granted, this aforementioned statement is complex, and when translated to the United States educational system, there are more things to consider, but broadly what holds true in truly any country, and in every classroom, is students will learn from a great educator.

As a high-performing individual and one who holds myself to high standards, I honestly hate to admit that I was not a great educator to all of my students in the same classroom and, perhaps, not even a good one to many. As a first-generation student, first daughter, and other things, I have a complex of perfection, and I have always wanted to get everything right. But I believe that highlighting the two different experiences my students had when I was their teacher will help draw the point of the special position of an educator.

Maria and Jose were both sweet and eager students in my class, and on the first day of their third grade year, I was ready to create an exhilarating environment of learning. My test drive as a fifth grade teacher the year before had taught me a few things, and I was excited about the possibilities of teaching, and truthfully, I thought it would be easier to teach a younger group of students. Immediately I learned that educating children in any grade was difficult and required a sophisticated set of skills. Educators have the opportunity to create a safe and nurturing learning environment for all of their students. My two young learners, Maria and Jose, had extremely different personalities like elements on a periodic table. One was like oxygen and the other one was hydrogen! Maria was an eager learner, hungry to take on the day's lesson and excited to raise her hand and respectfully engage in classroom participation. Jose was the opposite. He could not stay in his chair, would spontaneously blurt out responses, and would disrupt the learning environment. During the year, I significantly invested class time in Maria and other learners like her who were amenable to learning and following the rules I had set for the classroom. I wrote her little notes on her homework and test assignments, never missing an opportunity to lift up her brilliance and academic performance. Jose, on the other hand, received my less-than-qualified instruction and redirection of his attention to classroom instruction and rules. I often, perhaps daily, sent Jose to the office for his disruptive behavior. As a matter of fact, it was so bad that the administration had to set a meeting with me to inquire about the problem I was having with Jose. I was advised that none of his prior teachers or current elective teachers had this issue with Jose, and the administration was concerned about what was happening in my classroom. I committed to resolve the issue immediately, but the only resolution that I came to was not to send Jose to the office. But I continued to starve Jose of a rich learning experience because of my lack of training and inability to engage his attention as a learner in his classroom. I failed Jose and robbed his peers of his brilliance by not fostering an equitable learning environment that would meet him where he was and support him to develop his intellectual ability and curiosity. Instead of creating a connection with him, I wanted Jose to comply with the rules I had set for the classroom in order for me to release a quality learning experience for him. Maria, on the other hand, like other "well-behaved" students, received a premium learning experience from me to the point where just a few years ago, Maria had posted on her social media a picture of her in third grade with a measuring cup and next to it a screenshot of her final exam. On her final exam, there was a big "100, Great Job! The Scientist" and a smiley face in my handwriting. I sent her a quick note of encouragement that read, "You were destined for great things Maria, I knew that since I met you!!" She wrote back to share that she had chosen to pursue science as a career and also decided to share:

> Miss Marcela, you are going to make me cry!! Last semester I really doubted whether or not I made the right choice when choosing my career. Today I came across that paper and it was truly encouraging; it brought back great memories, and reminded me how much I've been wanting to be a scientist.

Thank you for your kind words, for encouraging me throughout all of these years, and being an inspiration to me.

This moment made me cry. I was very proud of the role I had played in the life of Maria, and with the same tears, I was disappointed in the role I had played in the life of Jose. I can't tell you what became of his future, but I am hopeful that I was just a terrible wrinkle in his academic journey and that other, more qualified and prepared educators, ironed out any and all harm I did to Jose's learning and development.

Educators play a special role in the life of children and can have a profound impact in their lives, and admittedly, this impact can be positive or negative if an educator is not equipped with the tools, talents, and resources they need in the classroom. For Maria, I unknowingly leveraged my special position in her life to lift her up both academically and with positive words of encouragement and support. In Jose's case, I took for granted the special position and opportunity I had as his teacher. I knew after my teaching experience that it takes a very special person to educate children in a very equitable manner and with a high degree of skill and that perhaps, with time, that could be me, but my time in Mexico would soon be coming to an end and I would return to my career, so I thought.

Unveiling the Evidence: The Special Position of Educators

Upon returning to the US, my career plans in insurance took an unexpected turn as I merged my business background with a newfound passion for teaching and learning. This life-altering shift propelled me on an extraordinary path to Harvard Graduate School of Education, where I was introduced to the ecological systems theory.

It was within the captivating classroom of Dr. Sara Lawrence Lightfoot, during her remarkable course "The Ecology of Education: Culture, Communities, and Change in Schools," that I embarked on a profound intellectual journey. The semester started with a learning journey of understanding "Ecological

Spheres and Frames." As we delved deeper into her book and the semester, we encountered Urie Bronfenbrenner's ecological systems theory. I was initially overwhelmed with the notion of a human development psychologist being intertwined with PK–12 academics, but as we delved into the theory and the profound impact of interactions among key stakeholders in a child's life, it became clear. Dr. Lightfoot's artful interpretation of his research illuminated the pivotal role played by educators in shaping the academic and human development of students as well as the interconnectedness of stakeholders to support students holistically. As our learning journey continued during the semester, we had the opportunity to read her book, *The Essential Conversation: What Parents and Teachers Can Learn From Each Other* which uplifted the idea around the power of relationships.

My comprehension and reflection on the ecological systems theory continues to grow, resonating profoundly with my personal journey as a student, educator, practitioner, and community member. The lessons I learned from studying Dr. Lightfoot's work as well as Bronfenbrenner's are abundant, and I wholeheartedly recommend immersing yourself in its pages if you haven't already had the chance. Bronfenbrenner's theory, as explained through Dr. Lightfoot's work, truly highlights the research that people other than biological parents have a special place in the lives of students. The ecological systems theory explains many complex ideas about human development much more than I will delve into in this book; however, in my opinion, it does a tremendous job in really highlighting the proximate nature of an educator in the life of a student. Educators have a special position in the lives of students. Understanding the special position of an educator in the life of a student is foundational to creating a deeper connection with students.

As a practitioner, I often use the aforementioned books and theories to help education leaders understand both the ecosystem of support that children have as well as the opportunities that exist to foster deep and meaningful partnerships among key stakeholders. In Figure 0.1 is an image we utilize to lift up the stakeholders, their proximity to an individual, and the relationships that could exist among each other.

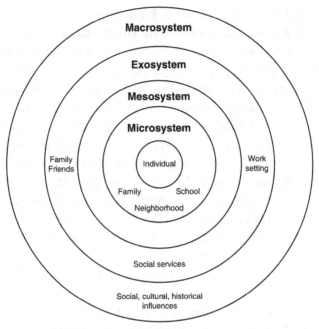

FIGURE 0.1 Urie Brofenbrenner's ecological systems theory.

What do you notice?

Ultimately, as you look at the Figure, it is clear that individuals are supported by their families, school, friends, and community—this system is referred to as the microsystem. The microsystem encompasses the key players closest to the lives of students who shape their experiences and growth. For educators, understanding their role in microsystems is crucial. It means recognizing that they are not just educating children but also playing a key role in their development. The way they interact, provide support, and create a positive learning environment for students directly impacts students' development. Educators have the power to inspire, nurture, and guide students within this special position.

When you look at the figure, you can see it includes the titles of individuals who are closest to a student and, thus, have an opportunity to hold a special position in their life to make an impact. And to be clear, just because you have the title doesn't give you the position—like everything in life, a position is earned. Thus, educators have the opportunity to have a special position in the lives of children, and it is fundamentally up to you what position you take. Even in the same classroom, during the same year, as an educator you can give children a completely different experience. In my own honest reflection of my practice as an educator, it wasn't the student, that is, Jose or Maria, that determined the special position I played in their life, it was the choices I made to act on my beliefs, mindsets, and behavior toward them—good or bad. We, too, were once children, and this theory also applies to how we learned and developed to the people we are today. The people who were most proximate to us had an impact on our lives, and the experiences we went through in life helped shape the beliefs, mindsets, and behaviors that we practice today. Put simply, we all went through our very own unique life experience surrounded by different people in different communities, and more than likely, there are significantly different values, beliefs, and practices that shaped who we are. Does it make it wrong? No, we are just different. And to truly be an effective educator, we must seek to understand, honor, and respect the different ecosystem of experiences that our students come from.

Beliefs, Mindsets, and Behaviors of Educators

What beliefs, mindsets, and behaviors do you have toward your students? Are they the same across the board? If not, why do you think that is?

In my work over the past few years, one concept that has surfaced as a possible reason why teachers hold certain beliefs, mindsets, and behaviors is simply because they are different from the students they serve and grew up with entirely different life experiences.

The majority of teachers in our schools today are White middle-class women, even when you look at schools that have an enrollment of students whose racial background is non-White. One thing I can further appreciate about Bronfenbrenner's work is that it helps us understand that each person, regardless of their race, ethnicity, or identity goes through life experiences that are not cookie-cutter, and they shape their development. I believe it is important to acknowledge that there is still much work to be done within our field to explore the consequences of these differences. One such consequence is the disproportionate impact of discipline and the school-to-prison pipeline. It is also essential to recognize and honor the unique truth that each individual holds regarding their own developmental journey. We must acknowledge that not everyone has had the same experiences or opportunities. By approaching these topics with sensitivity and understanding, we can foster a more inclusive and equitable environment and engage in reflection and dialogue about these important issues. In the interim, I encourage you to engage in a reflective exercise about the special place educators hold in the lives of children and how your own development impacts the mindsets, beliefs, and behaviors showing up in your practice.

When I think back to the educators who had the most impact on my life, I can see where they didn't take for granted their special position but, rather, used it to lift me up, love me, care for me, and ultimately contribute to the education I received to make me the person I am today even when they did not share the same racial or economic background. Mrs. Iris could have easily used her special position as an educator to shame me, punish me, and make me feel less than I already felt about myself, but instead, as you read in the preface, Mrs. Iris used her special position in my life to show compassion, love, and support, and that allowed me to feel safe in my learning environment and around her.

The Influential Role of Educators as Role Models and Mentors

In everyone's life there are people, beyond biological parents, who hold a very special position of access and have the potential to make a significant impact on their life outcomes. Chapter 5 will go into more depth to talk about how people in this special position can work together to have further collective impact, but in setting this foundation, I want to lean into the power that comes with this special position to do good or cause harm. Whether it is parents, family members, educators, doctors, or others in this privileged special position, if it is not handled with the care and attention it merits, it can have negative effects on a student, hence all the childhood trauma we hear of and many times triage in classrooms. The idea of educators holding a special position in the lives of children is foundational for the five principles to create deeper student connections. A stranger off the street may serendipitously impact the life of a student, but the position that teachers occupy, like other special stakeholders, in the life of a student automatically positions them to have a deeper impact.

***

I was absolutely thrilled and excited to enter my ninth-grade year at Pflugerville High School. There was so much gossip about how life would be when you were a *Pfish* in high school, and I was beyond ready for it. My friends and I would talk about what it would feel like to be in high school and vulnerably would share some of our fears. Since many of the students had grown up in the same town together, my biggest fear was that as we transitioned into high school, I would lose my new circle of friends and that I would have to start over again. The day came when we started our first day of high school. I was especially nervous for my track-and-field class because my family wasn't really into working out, and I had only just started running the year before during gym class with our coach, who was encouraging us to do distance runs on Tuesdays and Thursdays. My first day of track-and-field practice was for the books! Coach Marigold looked like a Barbie doll, and her personality was there to match it. She was married to the football coach, and they were a dynamic duo who kept the football and track teams in top shape. The first month of the class was fine. It took me a little while to remember to bring my water bottle, but I would soon make sure I packed it because regardless if we brought our water bottles or not, we still had to run the course. And Texas heat was no joke! One day we were training for a track meet and I was on my last two laps, but

I was feeling exhausted and a bit nauseous. Coach Marigold was on the side of the track timing each of our laps, and she noticed that I had significantly slowed down.

"Andrés, pick up the pace," she yelled.

I smirked when she called me by my last name because unlike my peers' last names, mine was often used as a first name, too, and I had previously asked her to call me Marcela.

"Coach, I am not feeling well," I yelled as I was starting to pass her by.

"Come on, Andrés, you have less than two laps to go. You got this. Remember pain is weakness leaving the body," she yelled as I picked up my pace.

"Pain is weakness leaving the body," I repeated over and over as I completed the rest of my two laps within my own personal record (PR) time.

All the girls were proud. We all managed to either beat or keep our PR time. After we finished cooling down, we started heading to the locker room to freshen up before the next class. Coach Marigold called me over. "Andrés, come over here for a minute," she requested.

I jogged slowly toward her, and she asked me, "What happened out there today?"

I told her that as I was running I started not to feel well as I was coming up on my last two laps.

"Why do you think you weren't feeling well? Describe your feeling," she asked me.

"Well, as I started to pick up my pace, I started having a pain on my right side, and it started hurting so bad that I thought I may need to throw up," I explained.

"How's your pain now that you've walked it off?" she inquired.

"Well, I don't actually feel anything right now. My pain is gone, and I don't feel like I need to throw up," I said.

"Ah, I see. So when you were running and pushing yourself harder, you started to have a pain on the right-hand side of your body, correct?" she asked.

"Yes. I was really trying to beat my PR, but it started to hurt too much," I said with a tone of disappointment.

"Well, you managed to stay within your PR time, so you should be proud of yourself," she said encouragingly.

"You know when I say pain is weakness leaving the body, it is for this exact moment. You had a side stitch because you were trying to break a new record. And in order for you to break a new record, you have to do a few different things when you are running," she started to explain. "You give the body the training it needs to go to the next level. If you want to go faster, you have to make some adjustments. During your next run, why don't you try to control your breath more and move your arms like you are hitting a wall with your elbows each time you take a step," she finished explaining.

"I think that probably would help. I'll give it a try." I was certainly not the fastest in my track class, but I was consistently breaking my own PRs, and with Coach Marigold's support and encouragement, it felt great!

Educators are role models and great mentors. During the year, Coach Marigold would mentor me and give me specific advice to improve my running. Additionally, everyone on our team adored Coach Marigold. She was tough with us, but she really challenged us to be our best self every day we got on that track. And the moments off the track, she would use to impart words of wisdom and lessons that we could apply to our lives.

Have you ever heard the phrase, *people know your glory, but they don't know your story*? The first time I heard the phrase, it deeply resonated with me.

As an educator, I think this holds true for you, too. People know that you educate children, but do they know the generational impact that you have on the lives of children and families? *Do you know?*

Unveiling the Impact: The Multifaceted Role of Educators in Society

In my journey going from poverty to prosperity, I have met so many amazing first-generation professionals who have an outlier story like mine. And without a doubt, the common denominator in their testimonies is an educator. Either an educator invested extra time with them, saw their creativity and helped them develop it, partnered with their families to navigate a system that was unfamiliar to them, helped them with college applications and scholarships, provided life advice, or, on the opposite side of the coin, harshly criticized and demoralized their development. The special position of an educator can go both directions, both positive and negative. For generations, educators have showed up for students beyond what their job descriptions say, and there are leaders all over the world that can testify to the power of an educator in their life. And as you have probably heard of in the news, some educators have negatively impacted the lives of children.

An educator is one of the most important people in the fabric of our society. Educators have a special position of power and privilege to teach and orient children to reach new horizons of their dreams and ultimately their fullest potential. Educators are part of a massive force of leaders who unselfishly invest their time and talent into developing the next generation of our society's citizens. From their work can come our nation's presidents, doctors, scientists, lawyers, astronauts, entrepreneurs, politicians, social media influencers, and more. The investment of talent educators make to our society literally builds the human capital engine that makes the world run.

Rewind. Grab a highlighter, your stickies, a camera, or whatever modern-day recording device you like and let's take extra note of the aforementioned sentence. This is one of the diamonds in this book and in your career I do not want you to miss. Educators make the world run, not just girls—sorry Beyoncé,[1] still your fan though!

Yeah, right, you are probably thinking. And if you look at how our society treats you, regards you, speaks about you, and makes decisions for you, I agree. As educators, you are, on average, overworked, underpaid, underappreciated, undertrained, and underprotected. It's disheartening that our society often views teaching as the easiest job, with summers off, as if it's "just" about teaching kids. Teachers in our country are not treated with the dignity and respect they deserve for the caliber of work and contribution they make to our society.

As a matter of fact, in writing this book, I had the opportunity to speak with many educators who shared their experiences and expressed their feelings of being disregarded and mistreated, especially in the post-pandemic era. They highlighted the increased behavior issues in classrooms, the rise in family complaints, and the overwhelming demands from administrators due to the strain of fully staffing schools. It is a challenging and often thankless job that requires immense dedication, perseverance, and resilience.

However, it is precisely because of these difficulties that the special position of an educator becomes even more remarkable and aspirational. Despite the obstacles, educators possess an extraordinary opportunity to make a profound impact on the lives of children. They have the power to inspire, motivate, and guide young minds toward their fullest potential. They hold the key to unlocking a student's curiosity, creativity, and confidence.

Educators can serve as role models and mentors, not only imparting knowledge but also instilling values, fostering growth, and nurturing a love for learning. They have the ability to create a supportive and inclusive environment where students feel safe, valued, and encouraged to explore their passions and dreams. By embracing their special position, educators have the potential to ignite a spark within each student, empowering them to believe in themselves and pursue their aspirations.

The impact of an exceptional educator extends far beyond the classroom walls. They play a vital role in shaping the future of our society by equipping students with the skills, knowledge, and character traits needed to become responsible citizens and future leaders. I can attest that the influence of a dedicated educator can ripple through generations, leaving a lasting legacy that extends far beyond the academic realm.

So, despite the challenges and the lack of recognition, let us celebrate the incredible potential and power that lies within the special position of an educator. Let us embrace the transformative capacity educators hold to shape lives, build communities, and inspire a brighter future for all.

Investing in Educators: A Crucial Priority

My mom loves to garden, and if you come over to my parents' home during the spring time and certainly before the scorching 100-degree weather, you will see lush green plants and trees everywhere. In particular, you will see several fig trees. One of my favorite pastimes with my mama is walking through her beautiful backyard and just talking about all things. Sometimes we talk about serious things, and other times we just catch one another up with things that are happening in our lives and the lives of our loved ones. But, without a doubt, there are several anecdotes that my mom will draw from when she is trying to emphasize a point. And there is one that seems very fitting to what is happening in education today. So many children, myself included, do not grow up the way our parents would dream for us to. If we were trees, anecdotally speaking, that would mean growing up slanted instead of straight. And many times my mom has pointed out that one of the reasons that trees are slanted is because of the conditions of their planting, in other words, the nutrients that ultimately made it or didn't make it to their roots or the exposure to the elements of water, sun, and air. She would proceed to tell me that how old and developed the tree is determines how much pressure you can apply to straighten it up. A newer, more tender tree's trunk is easier to straighten than an older, more mature tree. But she is always incredibly quick to say that a very slanted or crooked tree that is older and more mature cannot be straightened up drastically because in doing so, you break it; instead, she says, that you have to put the right supports along the tree so that it can start to take the slant that you desire. For example, it is easier to impact the formation of a young student than it is of a very well-established adult.

Our country is relatively new in comparison to other countries, and thus, our education system is also much newer than that of other countries. However, I fear that it is past its tender years and that if we try to straighten it up with drastic measures we will break it. Instead, I believe we need to start thinking about how we as a society can put the right supports around our education system tree and help it grow straight.

One strategy is certainly the level of investments we make in our educators. Educators have the noble and massive task of educating the next generation of leaders, and it is imperative that we make drastic changes to our public education system so that they can be respected and honored as the professionals they are and for the contributions that they make to our society.

And while this change transpires and we continue to see teachers leave the field of education in mass numbers, I offer a reflection. In taking Professor Marshall Ganz's, Rita E. Hauser Senior Lecturer, at Harvard Kennedy School, Public Narrative course, there were so many learnings about leading change during uncertain times.

During one of the first classes, he opened our time together with a quote from a first-century Jerusalem sage, Rabbi Hillel: "If I am not for myself, who will be for me? If I am only for myself, what am I? And if not now, when?" During the course of that class I remember thinking about all of the experiences I had lived through and how, in fact, there were things that I was both uniquely qualified as well as felt compelled to lead but didn't know how. Throughout the semester, I learned the importance of our own individual stories to drive change. Before, during, or after my birth, I didn't create a special request to be placed into the life circumstances that I was literally delivered into, but I have chosen to use my life circumstances to lead the life I have. You, too, I imagine, didn't put a request in to be placed in education during a very tumultuous time. *But if you are not a leader in education, then who? If not now, then when?*

And since we are on an existential note, let's engage in a classic compare-and-contrast activity. Take a moment to go back to Figure 0.1, and besides the microsystem that you just read about, take a moment to zoom out and observe the other systems. Notice the names of the other systems as well as what stakeholders and entities are represented. Also take note of the shape of the figure and the way the different systems are separated. In Figure 0.2, there is a picture of Earth's structure. Take a minute or two to take in the image. Now overlay the ecological system theory with Earth's structure and do a compare

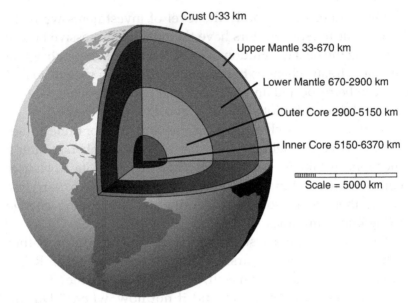

Crust 0-33 km

Upper Mantle 33-670 km

Lower Mantle 670-2900 km

Outer Core 2900-5150 km

Inner Core 5150-6370 km

Scale = 5000 km

FIGURE 0.2 Picture of Earth's structure

and contrast on the figures. What are similarities between the two figures? What are the differences?

Now forgive me for getting a little nerdy and existential with you for a minute—actually, don't forgive me, this is what great educators like you taught me to do! What did you notice and wonder about when you were doing the compare and contrast?

When I took in both figures, I noticed the microsystem is very similar to the center of our Earth. In fact, the closer I looked at it, the more I noticed that the microsystem is very similar to the inner and outer core of our Earth. Both figures show a multi-faceted interdependency that implies the connection is necessary for everyone to thrive on Earth as a community. I vaguely remember learning about Earth's structure in fifth grade using our earth science book and became curious and looked up what it had to say about the inner and outer core. Unfortunately, I wasn't able to find a copy but was able to use the internet's vast library to find an interesting fact about the inner and outer core that I didn't remember or perhaps never learned. According to Australian National University,[2]

> Despite its small volume (less than 1% of the Earth's volume), the Earth's inner core contains about 10% of the total magnetic field energy. It plays a crucial role in outer core liquid motions and the geodynamo, which generates the Earth's magnetic field. Without the magnetic field, life on Earth would be impossible.

Fascinating! I had to read that factoid multiple times, but ultimately, it mirrors exactly what Bronfenbrenner found in his research—the interconnected nature of our lives.

In and outside the classroom, educators have the opportunity to connect with students and their families to make a much deeper connection and impact their life outcomes. For students like me, who grew up in underprivileged communities, this means potentially having the opportunity to end generational poverty.

During the 2019–2020 school year, according to the National Center for Education Statistics (NCES),[3] "In the United States, the percentage of public school students who were eligible for free or reduced-price lunch, which is an indicator of poverty, was over 50%." Poverty directly affects educational outcomes, and educators in classrooms across the country hold a special position that can dramatically impact if students go from poverty to prosperity. And while educators are leaving the field in record numbers and I know our education system is currently erupting, I also know, through my own lived experience, the special place an educator holds in the lives of students.

As a society, we must make changes to support educators like you to fully leverage the special position you have in the lives of children to make a lifelong impact. It is imperative that we make drastic shifts to the mental models,[4] policies, and practices we have toward our educators. We must compensate educators equivalent to their investment into our society; we must equip and train them with all aspects of what it means to be an educator in America today; we must appreciate them way beyond a teacher appreciation week filled with goodies (although shout-out to principals and community members for those treats); and we must care for them as human beings. While, as a society, we work to make the aforementioned shifts, I offer this to every educator more directly: you were called for a time like this, under these circumstances and to support the children in our schools today to reach their fullest potential. Additionally, my dearest educators, I hope you truly know not only your collective power and influence over the lives of generations of students and families but also the role you play in society. Most classrooms have on average 20–25 students, although this number can vary. And even if as an educator you only served the same 20–25 students throughout your entire career, those 20–25 students represent 20–25 families whose lives you can impact through your special position.[5] But most educators have 20–25 students every year and with an average of about 14 years of tenure[6] (National Center for Education Statistics),[7] we are talking about 350 lives—that's arguably a community. Every teacher has the potential to impact not only their students but an entire community. Communities are what make up the very fabric of our society. In 2021, there were 3.2 million educators who impact the lives of over 49 million children and, thus, their families.[8] Educators not only have a special place in the lives of students, but they undoubtedly have their own personal power and collective power to impact the lives of children and our society.

Stacks of research will showcase how students living in poverty face much larger challenges than their peers. And while this is true we as a society speak to the pain point of our education system versus the possibility. Imagine what could be possible if every educator around the country made a deeper connection with their students, especially students who had disadvantages like poverty stacked against them. Imagine if every educator showed up like Mrs. Iris to educate the whole student or treated their students like I treated Maria and not Jose. Dare to imagine if educators walked in the same direction and lifted their collective voice demanding to be respected as the true professionals and contributors to our society that they are. My guess is that the teacher exodus would cease and there would be an explosion of professionals lining up at schools across the country wanting to use their talents to develop the next generation of leaders.

Educators are on the frontlines tasked with educating our nation's children, and they, better than anyone, know the stark reality of access to a high-quality education, let alone inequitable distribution of resources for students especially those living in high-poverty communities. They know that statistically students with deficit labels, like the ones placed on me, are pitted against structural and systemic barriers that will continue to cycle them into generational poverty. And for some, explicitly our young Black males, into the school-to-prison pipeline. With their eyes closed, educators can tell you which schools in a community are great and which ones are not serving students. As members of society, we all know this, too. Our education system is not currently designed to holistically support the students who live in high-poverty communities, communities that have a racial makeup of predominantly Black and Latino children. This holds true from the birth-to-career continuum. Currently our education system is also not designed to support most teachers working in high-poverty communities. Despite the challenges we see in our education system and regardless of the current demographics of teachers, it is my belief that most educators have a clear reason driving their career in education. And given the blatant inequities that start in our communities, I believe educators are motivated to create a more fair and just world for children by investing their time, energy, talent, and heart into the lives of students.

Educators play a pivotal role in shaping future generations, and they are uniquely positioned to make a difference in the lives of millions of children. Now, more than ever, they must deeply understand the position they hold in the lives of their students and our society. In case you didn't know the special position you hold in the lives of children, I hope this sets the foundation for five principles that I will share in the next few chapters to create a deeper connection with students.

Global Bright Spot of Encouragement

What educators described is nothing like what Pasi Sahlberg portrays about Finnish educators in *Finnish Lessons 3.0: What Can the World Learn from Educational Change in Finland?* Sahlberg highlights how Finland places a high value on teacher professionalism and expertise, where educators are respected as professionals in the field of education. In Finland, both educators and doctors are seen as highly respected professionals and undergo rigorous preparation and training to become highly qualified in their respective fields. They are required to meet high standards of education and expertise before practicing, and they are trusted to make decisions based on their knowledge and granted autonomy in their professions.

In contrast, educators in the United States are far from being regarded as true professionals. They are not compared to, paid, or regarded on the same level as doctors. According to the World Economic Forum,[9] the Finnish education system is globally recognized as one of the best. Two notable areas include student academic performance and the investment made in educators. Finland regards education as an honored profession and gives its educators the utmost trust, respect, and appropriate compensation they deserve.

It's disheartening to reflect on the fact that the GDP of Finland is approximately 78 times less than that of the United States, with a significantly smaller population size, yet they prioritize and value their educators to a much greater extent. As a society, we must question why we do not accord the same level of respect and compensation to our educators, despite having the resources to do so.

However, despite this stark reality, I know, without a doubt, that educators in Finland, in the US, and all over the world invest their time and talents into the next generation not solely for monetary gain but because they deeply understand that "Education, then, beyond all other devices of human origin, is the great equalizer of the conditions of men—the balance wheel of the social machinery," as the late secretary of education Horace Mann once stated.[10] While educators deserve to be paid well for their invaluable contributions, their dedication and passion stem from the transformative impact they have on the lives of children as witnessed through their own lived experiences. The profound impact educators have on the lives of children and their unwavering dedication remain the driving force behind their calling, and hopefully, one day, all countries can compensate educators according to their deep contributions to our world.

In the next chapter, we will get into the first key principle to foster deeper relationships with students in the classroom, and you guessed it, the first principle is all about you and what drives you—what is your *why*? In the meantime, I hope you profoundly understand the special place you have in the lives of children and the opportunity to make an impact and that now is when we need your leadership the most.

Five Key Affirmations for Educators to Remember

Educators hold a special place in the lives of students because they play a critical role in their education, serve as role models and mentors, create a safe and nurturing learning environment, support individual needs and differences, and shape our country's future citizens. The special position you hold extends beyond the classroom and impacts generations. I know this is a trying time to be in education, but since you are still here, I truly want you to know the role you play in the lives of students. In the next chapters, there will be five key practices you can adapt to your classroom context and setting to further connect with your students, but, for now, here are five key affirmations I want to make sure you know like the Pythagorean theorem! And I would truly love it if you put them on different colored Post-it notes on your bathroom mirror and remind yourself of them every day.

1. **As an educator, I play a critical role in my students'
development.** Educators play a crucial role in shaping a student cognitive, social, emotional, and physical development. Educators are responsible for imparting

knowledge, skills, and values that are essential for students to reach their fullest potential. Think about the impact Mrs. Iris had on my life in the way she approached my mistake with Mr. Slimy. Her guidance, support, and instruction left a profound and lasting impact on my growth and development. After all, I don't steal snails anymore!

2. **As an educator, I am a role model and mentor.** Educators often serve as positive role models and mentors for their students. The life experiences and anecdotes educators share when bringing their full selves into the classroom don't go unnoticed, and students listen to your stories and advice. Like Coach Marigold, educators exemplify positive behaviors, attitudes, and values and can inspire and motivate students to strive for excellence, overcome challenges, and pursue their passions. Educators can also provide guidance and mentorship, offering valuable advice and support that can help shape children's character, resilience, and self-esteem. Every time I do something hard I continue to repeat to myself, pain is weakness leaving the body!

3. **As an educator, I impart knowledge for students to reach their fullest potential.** Educators create a safe and nurturing learning environment where students can grow in their thinking, learn new ideas, and thrive to new levels. Teaching is your craft, and you have a unique set of skills and passion to lead the work that you do. When you are inside of a classroom, you are teaching a curriculum, you are providing valuable lessons students can use inside and outside the classroom, and you are also modeling how to masterfully share your talent with the world.

4. **As an educator, I have the ability to support every student in their journey.** Educators recognize and support the individual needs and differences of children. Educators create inclusive classrooms where all children, even the rambunctious ones that are like

hydrogen, feel valued, respected, and supported.
Educators use their special position to provide emotional support, create a sense of belonging, and foster a
positive classroom culture that can enhance children's
well-being and sense of security. The environment
I created for Maria should be the same I should have
created for all of my students.

5. **As an educator, I play a pivotal role in shaping future generations.** Oh my dear educators, I wish there were
billboards flashing neon lights that showcase to the
world the significant impact you have on developing
future generations. The work you lead directly impacts
our future. Educators plants seeds of knowledge, skills,
and values that shape students' attitudes, beliefs, and
behaviors as they grow into adulthood. You truly,
truly have the opportunity to instill a lifelong love for
learning, critical thinking skills, and a sense of social
responsibility in children, which can have far-reaching
effects on their future success and contributions to
society.

Reflection Questions for Introduction—The Special Position of an Educator

1. How did an educator positively impact your life during
your childhood, and how did they establish a meaningful
connection with you?
2. As an educator, what unique role do you believe you play
in the lives of children, and how do you strive to make a
difference?
3. What do you find to be the most significant challenge in
building strong connections with your students, and why
do you think it is difficult to overcome?
4. What specific training or professional development
opportunities would you like to receive in order to
enhance your ability to connect with and positively
impact the lives of your students?

Notes

1   Beyoncé is the recording artist for "Run the World (Girls)."
2   The Australian National University. (n.d.). *Research School of Earth Sciences*. In *The Earth's Inner Core*. ANU Research School of Earth Sciences. https://earthsciences.anu.edu.au/earths-inner-core
3   National Center for Education Statistics. (2023). Concentration of public school students eligible for free or reduced-price lunch. In *Condition of Education. U.S. Department of Education*. Institute of Education Sciences. https://nces.ed.gov/programs/coe/indicator/clb
4   Mental models are how the mind represents real, remembered, hypothetical, or imaginary situations.
5   https://nces.ed.gov/surveys/ntps/tables/ntps1718_fltable06_t1s.asp
6   https://www.nea.org/nea-today/all-news-articles/who-average-us-teacher
7   https://nces.ed.gov/fastfacts/display.asp?id=372
8   https://nces.ed.gov/fastfacts/display.asp?id=372
9   https://www.weforum.org/agenda/2016/11/finland-has-one-of-the-worlds-best-education-systems-four-ways-it-beats-the-us
10   http://www.caggiasocialstudies.com/docs/AH104/Mann

1

Principle 1: Know Your Why

When driving in a large urban city, I rely on my GPS to navigate the unfamiliar exits and roads. My sense of direction often fails me, and it's easy to find myself on an entirely different journey with just a blink of an eye. Similarly, in the vast and quickly changing landscape of education, knowing your *why* is like having a personal GPS for your purpose. As an educator, understanding your why becomes the driving force (pun intended) behind the deep connections you establish with students. It also really helps to avoid deep personal frustration as what happens when I take the same wrong exit for the millionth time.

Growing up, my family and I lived in an apartment complex that was next to two unfenced commercial trash cans on a street that was considered the most dangerous in our city because of the amount of violence, gang affiliation, prostitution, and other serious crime offenses that happened there. My parents immigrated to the United States from two different countries seeking a better life. My mother immigrated from Atotonilco, a small town in the state of Zacatecas, in Mexico, and my father immigrated from Havana, Cuba. Like many immigrants with little money, they started out where they could with what they had. And in their case, they accepted to live with one of my aunts and uncles until they were somewhat financially stable and could live on their own. My father had left Cuba as a political refugee, and my mother left Mexico because of extreme poverty. While things went seemingly well for my parents at the beginning of

DOI: 10.4324/9781003401018-2

their marriage, when I was five years old, my parents separated. When my father left, my mom spoke very little English, didn't have a car, relied on a middle-school level education, and soon would have three mouths to feed because she was eight months pregnant with my little sister.

My first year of kindergarten was challenging. My father was gone, and I rarely saw my mother because she was working all the time to do everything she needed to do to make sure we had all the basic necessities to live. My mother had just given birth to my little sister and immediately had to take on multiple jobs to provide for us in addition to taking on a roommate to help pay for the bills. But, from the moment I started kindergarten, I loved school!

My classroom was beautiful, colorful, and clean. There were more books that I had ever seen in a garage sale (where we usually bought our books), and there was this feeling of calm and protection inside the classroom. And my teachers were so nice even though most of them looked very different from me as most were White. This was true for most of my K–12 journey. Although my teachers never directly addressed me with harsh words, my identity was labeled with words such as "at-risk," "English-language learner," "economically disadvantaged," "single-parent household," and "minority." *Que bueno que no hablaba bien el inglés,*[1] and that educators never used those words directly at me; otherwise, those words would have crushed my little spirit. When I was in seventh grade, my mom remarried, and we moved to a new city not too far from Austin, Texas, and into a house where I would have my very own room for the first time in my life.

Despite the trash cans, despite the labels, and despite always eating off-brand cereals with no toy as the prize, my story is one that went from poverty to prosperity. I grew up in the "hood" of my small city and moved to a small town 15 minutes away where I would later graduate from high school. I was supposed to go to the U.S. Naval Academy after receiving the congressional nomination from one of our state representatives, but ultimately I went to Saint Edward's University (SEU). I graduated SEU with a bachelors of business administration with a concentration in finance and years later pursued a master's in education from Harvard Graduate School of Education. I have traveled the world and now own a consulting firm on a mission to reimagine how educators, families, and communities partner to support the hopes and dreams of children.

In college, if you had asked me what my why was, I would have simply shared that I wanted to make a lot of money because growing up I didn't have any. Today, after a nonlinear, unplanned, and unconventional path, I can confidently say my why is ending generational poverty through high-quality education coupled with the deep human connections between individuals who love students most.

Knowing your why is sometimes a journey. Unknown to me, my why was being shaped as I first entered K–12 school, remained surface level for most of my undergraduate studies, and really emerged as I started and continued my career. It is because of K–12 educators like you and the circle of support that worked together to support, monitor, and advocate for my dreams that I am here today writing this book and that fuels my why.

During university, as I got closer to graduation, the preliminary whimpers of my why came to life during the writing of my capstone thesis paper. My peers were writing about mergers and acquisitions and delving into other seemingly more directly related topics to finance, but I wanted to write about *Brown vs. Board of Education* and the inequality of education, especially the experiences of Black and Brown students that came from communities like the one I had grown up in. Perhaps it was that many students at my university didn't share my racial or economic background or the fact that I knew my childhood classmates had taken a polar opposite life journey, but something was unsettled within. The muffled whispers of my why would become much clearer through a series of events and much deeper investigative process later in my life. After I graduated from SEU, I found myself working for the same large insurance company I started working for when I began studying at the university. Even though I enjoyed writing my capstone and had learned a lot of the inequalities that persist in schools, my why remained to make money. Through my networks I had learned about real estate, and in addition to working in insurance, I earned a real estate license to become a REALTOR®. I was doing pretty well, actually. All things considered, I was doing great! I bought my first house shortly after graduating college and had a master plan to make tons of money with both insurance and real estate.

And then came the nonlinear.

Life happened, and I took a sabbatical to live in my mother's home country, Mexico. While living in Mexico, the muffled whimpers of my why started to become a soft whisper that said, "Education is your why." Since my plan was originally to only live in Mexico for three years, I decided to take a small break from insurance. As my three-year sabbatical was coming to an end, so was my time in the classroom. Although I thoroughly enjoyed my role as a teacher, I knew that it took a very special person to be in the presence of children and create an environment of deep learning. Don't get me wrong, I definitely had some strengths as a teacher, but I think you know and, more importantly, the students know that when a teacher knows their why, the teaching is different. Just ask Maria and Jose. I was certainly not skilled to bring out the brilliance and genius in all students equitably.

After working in Mexico for three years in education, I returned back to Austin to resume my career in insurance. I had enjoyed my time in the classroom but believed that teaching was not for me, so I would seek to return to my career in insurance. But something was different—I was different. As a bilingual Latina who held a bachelor's in business administration and had a strong background in insurance, I was poised very nicely to return to insurance and started looking at the career paths available. I came across a recruiter and was immediately drawn in by an opportunity that seemed to be once in a lifetime. The recruiter told me about an opportunity to open up my own insurance agency. She shared that because of the continued growth in the Hispanic market and the projected growth they were expecting in Manor, a small town north east of Austin, the company was actually looking for a candidate that spoke Spanish and understood the Hispanic market. Check, I thought. Additionally, if selected, I would receive a nice compensation and start-up package equating to a little over a quarter million dollars. Sign me up, I thought! The only challenge was that it would take about 6–8 months to go through the process, but she basically guaranteed me that I would get the spot given my experience and credentials. I felt very confident that this opportunity would be mine, so I started the application process to apply for my own insurance agency.

But then life had other plans. Doesn't it always?

While I was going through the lengthy vetting process with the insurance company, I serendipitously found an operations opportunity posted on a Craigslist job board at a large charter school network. I had absolutely no clue what a charter network was or the reform movements that were happening in education, but something about the job really caught my attention. Ultimately, I resolved that I needed to have a plan B in case the insurance pathway didn't work out. But honestly, its mission deeply resonated with me. Its mission strongly asserted that zip codes shouldn't define destiny. I knew this was true, in theory, but in my lived experience, it wasn't the case. Zip codes did and still do define the destiny of student outcomes.

My draw to the mission of the charter network and my plan B for another job in case I didn't get the insurance agency landed me in a little predicament. I was ultimately made a job offer for both the insurance agency and the charter network! The decision to open two schools as a founding operations manager of a growing charter network versus opening my own agency with a large insurance company was a difficult decision I had to make in my life. The offers were seemingly quite different. One opportunity offered exponential growth in my promising insurance career along with the potential of making a lot of money during my lifetime, and I mean a lot—so much I could buy all the cereal boxes I wanted with toys inside! And the other offered the opportunity to be part of something bigger than me, with very little compensation in return, but to make a difference in the lives of students, students who looked like me and shared a similar background. When comparing the two opportunities, I saw how both would put me in a position to underwrite some of the biggest risks in American society. One as an underwriter insuring risk and the other as a leader in the education system supporting the learning and development of the next generation.

So how did I decide to take and stay on the path of education? *My why.*

Days prior to accepting one role and turning down the other, I overheard my *mama* say to one of my *tias,* "*Muchas veces nos enfocamos en mejorar nuestras propias circunstancias pero se nos olvida mirar hacia atrás y echarle la mano a los que vienen detrás.*"[2] I was in the guest bedroom, but although I knew she wasn't talking to me, I knew the message was for me. As a woman of faith, I, along with my small church group, had been praying for my life's direction. Living in my mother's home country really had an impact on my life, and I wanted to make sure that as I pursued my career, I was very thoughtful with how I was investing my time and talents. The decision to pursue a career that would give me and my family the financial freedom that I only heard of in movies or instead pursue a career in education was a difficult one.

In her non-talking, talking to me, my mother basically said that we get too caught up in focusing on our own wins and we forget to look back at others who are coming behind us and lifting them up to where we are. And she was right. I knew from the moment I heard her, what my choice would be. After prayer, I affirmed what for a long time was struggling within me to be uttered: *my why.* My why was to work against educational inequity because I was living proof of what was possible when families, educators, and community members support students. Living in poverty was a climb; the restrictions on the foods I could eat, clothes I could wear, activities I could engage in were limiting; the safety outside and sometimes inside my apartment were very challenging; the trauma I experienced was damaging, and the list goes on. But in that moment, I could see that my life was proof of the research that demonstrates when students have access to high-quality education and a strong circle of support they are more likely to thrive.

In that season of pivot, it became clear to me that I was born for a purpose beyond making money and I had a responsibility to uplift the challenges and barriers that students who live in communities like the ones I grew up in face to navigate out of generational poverty. From my lived experience in poverty, to writing about inequity in my undergraduate capstone, and living in Mexico and working as a classroom teacher, I owed it to my community to look back and authentically share my voice and experience of the struggle. And I knew, without a doubt, I especially owed it to the students who came from the communities that I came from to be part of the cadre of change agents that are working to make education more accessible and equitable to all. When I accepted the role in education, I knew things would be hard because I didn't formally study education, but when things get difficult on this journey, I always go back to my why.

In fact, my career pivot was one of the most rewarding and significant things I have done in my life. Given my life journey, I simply was not going to be able to invest my time and talent into anything else but working in the education space. Once I made the decision to work in education, I knew *my why* was in alignment with *my work*. Every time I walk into a classroom and see the magic that happens between an educator and a student, I know that I made the right decision to invest my time and talent into education.

When I was presented with two career opportunities, one paying a quarter of a million and the other paying a quarter of that, one would think the choice would be clear and easy. But just like the thousands of educators feeling pressed with the decision to either stay in the classroom or exit the field of education, I felt like the pay was not the only factor but rather something much bigger and more complex than money, *my why*. What is *your why*?

Principle 1: Know Your Why

When you know your why and are aligned with your purpose, you show up differently. Knowing why you work in education can help fuel your passion, empathy, and unwavering commitment to making a positive impact in the lives of your students. It becomes the guiding voice (the purpose GPS) that leads you to create a meaningful, rich, and high-quality learning environment where students feel truly welcomed, heard, and inspired. If I had been clear on my why when I was teaching third and fourth grade, my students and I would have had a totally different experience.

Understanding your why is the first principle of deeper student connections. Education was not something I intended to dedicate my time and talents to, but I am honored that in my life journey, it chose me. When educators know and operate from their why, their practice looks and sounds differently. Think back to the educators that you have had in your life. Like me, I think you would be able to identify the educators who led with their why very easily. Mrs. Iris was clearly one of those. Students who have educators that lead with their why get to enjoy the reverberation of learning notes that just hit the soul differently. When educators operate from their why, students receive a very different learning experience.

A few years ago, I went to visit some of my dear friends who I met while I was in graduate school, and they invited me to attend an event at the Boston Philharmonic. The event was packed, but my friends and I somehow managed to get a seat up front. I had never heard about conductor Benjamin Zander, but the moment I saw his ability to guide students to draw out their musical abilities I was further inspired with this notion of using your why. During our time there, within minutes, I saw and heard the significant musical growth with all of his students. Because I was so in awe of the magic that was taking place, I managed to record one of his interactions with his student. Zander called the student to the stage and instructed him to start playing a piece on the violin. The student started playing, and you could see on Zander's face that he was going to interrupt the student shortly. What I noticed is what Zander calls out when he interrupts the student. The student was meekly looking at his violin as he started playing, and when Zander stopped him, he told the student to not look at his violin but rather to look at his audience instead and tell a story. He told the student to make a connection with the audience and get to know us because we had come from far to see him.

I was enthralled by the connection between the student and his teacher. It was clear to me that the conductor was leading from a place of why, and because he led from a place of knowing his why, he inspired his student to lead from a very different place, too.

It was exhilarating to watch how the student progressed from a meek violin player to a confident and very talented violin player within minutes. The interaction between the conductor and student was captivating. Zander would make hand motions and sounds to continue signaling to his student to perform from a different level, and with each note, the student's musical expression was much more clear and audibly pleasing. When Zander noticed the student's face turning into the violin, he would overexcitedly motion to the student to look at the audience, and then, with vigorous hand motions, he would instruct the student to play the violin with more intensity. As the student continued to play, Zander used fewer and fewer words to instruct the student, and as you can imagine, there was this amazing finale where the student nailed every single note as if he himself were the composer of the piece!

If a non-educator came into your classroom, what would they experience? Would they see an educator who is leading with their why and guiding their students to perform from a different level? Would they see a student's talents erupting after the dynamic instruction and guidance from their educator? More importantly, when you reflect on your practice, what grade would you give yourself in leading from your why? We tend to be our harshest critic, and the benefit of that is we can also use that self-assessment to grow in our practice.

Why did you make the choice to become an educator? The real deep why?

What is your why? Why do you do the work you do? What makes you physically get out of bed, run your morning routine, and show up to invest your time, talent, joy, and 40 plus hours of your weekly life into educating the next generation? At what moment in your life did you know that investing your time and talents in educating the next generation was something that filled you with purpose? If it's not that for you, then what is the driving force behind your choice to be an educator?

There is a moment, or a series of moments, in your life's journey that shaped your mind and heart to do the work that an educator does. And you and I both know that it isn't the money. Now don't get me wrong, we as a society need to fix that as I stated earlier—we need to have much better pay for educators and better working conditions. But to be clear, educators don't educate because of the salary they make; they educate because of their why.

What is your why?

Especially as we see an exodus of teachers leaving the field in droves, what brought you to teaching? If you are not yet in the classroom, why do you want to teach? Your why is what will fuel you when things get difficult.

And things are difficult now.

And I get it. Like I truly, truly get it. As you are reading this book, you, too, may be considering leaving the field of education, and I don't blame you—it's very hard to be an educator right now. But if I may, I want to motivate you to see a different possibility.

From my experience of living in poverty to my current experience of being a self-funded entrepreneur, I understand struggle, I understand pain, I understand pressure, and I understand how it feels to want to give up. But I chose not to let poverty define my future, and I am constantly choosing not to let the systemic barriers that I face as a Latina entrepreneur dictate how I will lead my life and where I will invest my time and talents. I'm kicking off my fourth year in business, and I can tell you that this entrepreneurial journey has been hard. But I choose not to give up because of my why.

One of my favorite examples of embracing your why is a short three-minute viral YouTube video by comedian Michael Jr. If you have a moment, check it out. Until the writing of this book, I always thought this video clip came from a comedy library, but was shocked to learn that Michael has used this video to also share his faith during services at Life Church.[3] And even more shocked that he references my favorite bible verse, Jeremiah 29:11. In his video, Michael explains to his viewers that "when you know your why, your what has more impact because you are walking in or towards your purpose.[4]" I LOVE this video! My short written summary will do it no justice so I highly recommend you watch it. One of the key moments I enjoy is when Michael asks an audience member to sing "Amazing Grace," and after a few stanzas, Michael interrupts him and asks him to re-sing the song, but this time asks him to remember he and his family have overcome some challenging circumstances, and immediately, you can notably see and hear the difference between the delivery of the song from the participant. The depth and emotion which the audience member pours into the song significantly changes when Michael asks him to sing from a different place, from his why. It gets me teary-eyed every time! I love using this short video when we kick off a new project with our clients because it gives a visual example of the power of knowing your why. After watching the video, we all take turns to share our why. This activity allows us to connect as human beings and not just get down to business as usual but rather deeply understand the lens we are coming in with for our partnership.

Another great resource is Simon Sinek's *Start With Why: How Great Leaders Inspire Everyone to Take Action*; the book's concept is also very similar to Michael's message. In his book, Sinek highlights several leaders who exemplify this very same principle of starting with your why, the deeper purpose and driving motivation behind your actions and decisions. These leaders include Steve Jobs, the co-founder of Apple, who went beyond just selling us all the apples that fall from under the tree (iPads, iPhones, iPencils, etc.) by selling us an idea that we could have a portable computer at our tiny fingertips. And Reverend Martin Luther King, Jr., a renowned civil rights activist and leader, who was known for his determination to fight for freedom and equal rights during the Civil Rights Movement for Black Americans. Also, Sinek highlights the Wright Brothers, Orville and Wilbur, who, thanks to their vision that human flight in the air was possible, are the reason why we have millions of planes flying around the world today. While each of these mentioned are now famous for the realization of their visions, my guess is that when they weren't so famous, they found inspiration to show up and persist from their deeper purpose and motivation—their why.

Five Practices to Leverage Your Personal Why

By leveraging your personal why, you can infuse your teaching with purpose, meaning, and authenticity. This can result in more effective teaching practices, stronger connections with students, and a greater sense of fulfillment in your role as an educator. As I have evolved in my practice as a consultant and, dare I say, a change agent who envisions reimagining the family engagement model, I have noticed the exchange of humanity that happens when we open up about the driving reason(s) that propel our work. We have all gone through life experiences that have shaped the persons and professionals we are today. And while, oftentimes, it may be a little uncomfortable to share with the world the difficult and sometimes challenging circumstances we lived through that drive the reasons why we do the work we do, the release of that why in our practice has a profound effect on us and a ripple effect on others. This is also true if you have come from a very privileged place. Sharing with individuals, especially strangers, what drives you is not always comfortable. Knowing your why, embracing it, and modeling for students really gives you the opportunity to shine your gifts to the world and for others to have permission to shine their gifts, too.

As you consider and define your personal why, I encourage you to lean into your stories, and if you are like me and find it challenging to articulate your why, seek coaching. Your students will absolutely know when you are operating from a place of why, and it will allow you to make a deeper connection with yourself and your students. Next are five practices you can use to find your way.

1. **Engage in reflective journaling/meditation/prayer:** Take time to engage in one or all of these reflective approaches to explore your lived experiences that have impacted your decision to pursue education. Consider reflecting your past experiences, both positive and challenging, and extract meaningful insights from them. I highly

recommend doing this practice especially after you watch the Michael Jr. video.

2. **Reflect on personal values and beliefs**: Understanding your personal why can help you align your teaching practices with your core values and beliefs and infuse your teaching with purpose and meaning. Consider engaging in a short activity to reflect and write down your personal values and beliefs about education and teaching. What values and beliefs do you have about education? Why?

3. **Share personal stories**: Stories are incredibly powerful and have been used for years to share important messages and lessons. Invest time to take inventory of stories that have taken place in your life and create a space to share those personal stories and experiences to connect with your colleagues, families, and students on a deeper level. Sharing personal anecdotes, challenges, and successes can make teaching more relatable and humanize the learning experience. It can also create opportunities for others to see you as a real person with unique perspectives and backgrounds, foster a sense of connection and trust, and ultimately help others understand what shapes your why.

4. **Listen to podcasts/read books**: The practices of leading with your why have been widely known and researched. Consider taking time to find other resources like Simon Sinek's book or Michael Jr.'s YouTube video to improve your skill of identifying, sharing, and leveraging your way. Additionally, there are tons of podcasts that talk about this idea of purpose and leading with your why.

5. **Advocate for change**: Your personal why can inspire you to advocate for change in your school, district, or educational system. You can use your voice and influence to advocate for policies, practices, and resources that align with your why and can positively impact student learning. This might involve speaking up at staff meetings, engaging in professional development opportunities, or collaborating with colleagues to drive change at a systemic level.

Novela Feature Case Study: Educators Leverage Their *Why* to Create a Deeper Connection With Students

Background: Ms. Moore had been appointed the new grade-level chair for sixth grade, and although she was excited for her new role, she was also very nervous. It was the beginning of the new school year, and many teachers had left the previous year as a result of a change in administration. Her colleagues were mainly new first-year teachers who didn't share the same racial or economic background of their students. The school was nestled in a lower-socioeconomic community that had food deserts, and the majority of students were either Black or Latino.

Challenge: A few months into the school year, Ms. Moore noticed that her weekly professional development sessions with her colleagues were becoming more tense. Her peers would arrive late and often be on their devices when she was giving training on how to improve classroom engagement. One day as she was going about her lesson, one of the educators interrupted her.

"What is the point of this PD? No matter what we try, the students don't care about learning. They come to class late, and when they are in class, they are often disruptive and very rude," Mr. Greg said.

"Yeah, it's like we are forcing them or even punishing them to be here in class. Oftentimes, my kids roll their eyes at me when I try to command their attention," Ms. Smith chimed in.

"Well, at least you haven't gotten something thrown at you or have been hit," said Ms. Guiterrez.

"I don't think I can teach here much longer. I've been in education for 10 years now, but kids are just not the same after COVID. I too feel like there are more behavior issues and lack of engagement when I am trying to teach the curriculum," shared Ms. Martin with the group.

The timer went off indicating the PD session was over. Ms. Moore felt deflated and told everyone that next week they would resume the conversation as it was apparent that everyone had a lot to share. But she was perplexed. How was she going to support her new teachers and even some of her more veteran teachers with some of the issues they were facing? The school culture and climate were certainly different since the pandemic, and everything her colleagues had shared resonated with her.

Application of Principle 1:

Then it dawned on Ms. Moore that the next PD session she could lead was to support her peers in grounding themselves with why they decided to be educators in the first place. Ms. Moore took note that everyone seemed to be deflated, and while she understood that everything they had shared needed to be addressed, what she saw was that teachers were not speaking or operating from their highest self. In sharing their challenges, their choice of words had a lot of deficit framing and a lot of onus placed on the student.

During the next PD, Ms. Moore showed Michael Jr.'s "Know Your Why" video. After showing the video, she first modeled the activity they were going to engage in by sharing her why. Then she gave everyone two minutes to jot down their thoughts and reflections on their why and encouraged them to be prepared to share their why in three to five minutes like she had. Everyone took turns sharing their why, and at the end of the activity, Ms. Moore had learned so much more about her colleagues, even Ms. Martin whom she had known for 10 years already. Some of her colleagues shared that they had gone into education because they had lived a privileged life and felt like they wanted to give back through education; one educator said she loved to get summers off and really loved working with students; a couple of educators shared that growing up, being an educator was all they ever dreamed of doing since they came from a line of educators; one educator shared that he decided to invest his talents in education because he had a really hard upbringing and there were very few people that helped him out, but that he had had the support of a teacher that really believed in him. As the PD session started coming to an end, Ms. Moore asked everyone to tap into their why during the next week as they were working with students and if they felt comfortable enough even to share with students their why. The next week, PD was on fire. The energy was just different. All the teachers seemed to have grown a little closer, and they were excited to share the impact the PD had on their practice and in their classroom.

Impact on Students:

Building Relationships:
The educators shared that students loved hearing their why and that it helped them build stronger relationships with their students. Additionally, by sharing their why, the educators reported that they were able to create a safe and inclusive space where students felt comfortable sharing their thoughts, ideas, and emotions, leading to a deeper connection and trust.

Empowerment and Student Voice:
The activity had been so successful in their PD that many of the educators modified the activity and asked students in their classroom to share what they wanted to be when they grew up. And just like Ms. Moore had modeled, the educators also asked students to lean into sharing the why driving their future aspirations. Not only did it give all the

students the opportunity to use their voice and share about their dreams, it also provided students a sense of ownership and pride in their education, creating a deeper connection and investment in their learning journey.

Summary

In this case study, Ms. Moore, the grade-level chair for sixth grade, faces the challenge of disengaged students and frustrated teachers in a school with a predominantly Black and Latino student population. To address this, she leads a professional development session centered around educators reconnecting with their why. By sharing their personal motivations and aspirations, the teachers develop a deeper understanding of each other and build stronger relationships with students. This leads to a more inclusive and empowering learning environment, where students feel comfortable sharing their dreams and aspirations. The activity sparks a positive shift in teacher-student dynamics, fostering deeper connections and increasing student engagement and ownership in their education.

Reflection Questions for Chapter 1—Principle 1: Know Your Why

1. How can you ensure that you are truly connecting with your students on a human level and understanding your why as an educator in order to foster trust and rapport in your classroom, create a supportive and safe environment, and encourage students to express themselves, ask questions, and take risks in their learning journeys?

2. How can you connect with your educator colleagues to learn about their why and share your why to help foster a sense of community?

3. How do you intentionally align your personal values and beliefs with your teaching practice in order to create a more meaningful and impactful learning experience for your students?
4. What strategies or techniques do you use to consistently remind yourself of your personal why as an educator, and how does this awareness influence your decision-making in the classroom?

Notes

1   It's a good thing I didn't speak English well.
2   *Many times we focus on improving our own circumstances but we forget to look back and lend a hand to those who come behind.*
3   https://www.life.church/media/punchline/punchline/
4   https://www.youtube.com/watch?v=1ytFB8TrkTo

2

Principle 2: Understand Context Beyond Compliance

The movement of ocean waves with a light mist of the waters hitting your face is so relaxing and rejuvenating that if I could spend more time at the beach, I certainly would. During a recent trip to South Beach, Florida, my mom and I were sitting on the white sandy beach near the shore, taking selfies with psychedelic glasses we had bought that afternoon from a local souvenir shop. It was our own little photo session, celebrating life and taking in time together. As the day started coming to end, we were both excited to visit a local establishment that was playing live music while we enjoyed dinner. While we were looking over the menu, my throat started to itch, and I could feel it constricting a little. I began coughing gently, but by the time the server was taking our order, I had to ask that they bring me hot tea with honey—quite the pairing with my sea bass dinner plate. Before the waiter could return, my cough got even worse, and I was really struggling to breathe. Thankfully, the tea seemed to settle the itch in the back of my throat, and we were able to finish our dinner and enjoy the band playing their ensemble.

We returned to our Airbnb, and my uncle who lives in Miami stopped by to visit and say hello. We enjoyed each other's company and caught up with all the things he was enjoying about living in Miami, especially that the culture in the city had many people making top investment in their personal beauty and care.

DOI: 10.4324/9781003401018-3

Since he is an aspiring photographer, he was excited about all of the doors that were opening for him to pursue photography further. We invited him to come out with us to the beach the next day as it was set to be an absolutely beautiful day, and with clear skies, I imagined that the sunset was going to be majestic. He agreed and said that he'd be back in the morning so we could all hang out for the entire day.

As we were saying our goodbyes, I started coughing again. This time the cough made it unbearably difficult to breathe, and my uncle offered to go to the local pharmacy to buy me some cough drops and syrup to soothe my throat. I felt bad since he was on his way out, but he said not to worry about it because we are family and that he wanted to make sure I was okay. Both he and my dad went to the pharmacy and returned with cough drops and cough syrup. Almost immediately I started feeling better after taking the cough syrup they had brought from the pharmacy, and shortly after, I fell asleep in my room while my parents and my uncle stayed in the living room watching a movie on Netflix. It probably wasn't more than an hour that I had fallen asleep when the cough came back, and again I found it difficult to breathe. So I took another cough drop, but this time, I noticed that it wasn't helping me like it did the first time. I fell back asleep thinking that perhaps just resting and making it through the night would make me feel better. Unfortunately, around midnight, I woke up again. This time with a violent cough that made it nearly impossible to breathe. My mom came into my room and said that we needed to go into the emergency room, that the cough sounded really bad, and that it even hurt her when I would cough. She said that my uncle would take us. She shared that after I fell asleep, he had decided not to leave until he was sure that I wouldn't need to go to the hospital. With tons of resistance, I finally obliged, mostly because my uncle had stayed for this exact reason, even though, at first, I found it silly to go to the emergency room for a persistent cough. Prior to going to the hospital, I sucked on another cough drop and took another dose of the cough syrup. While waiting for the attending physician, my cough started to subside a little, and I fell asleep. When finally the doctor came into the emergency room, my cough had almost stopped, and just as I had feared, the doctor looked at me with eyes that I translated to judgment for coming in for a silly cough. Dr. Fin looked at his notes, looked at me, and without testing me, made the determination that I had COVID. I pushed back and said I didn't have COVID as I had just taken a test. I tried to explain my symptoms, but instead, he looked at his chart and again said I had COVID. With a little frustration in my voice, I asked Dr. Fin, "So what happens if you test me and I don't have COVID?" Dr. Fin did not appreciate my dissenting comment and looked at the nurse and requested that they do a COVID test on me. A few hours later, Dr. Fin came back with the nurse and the COVID results and confirmed that, in fact, I did not have COVID. With no apology or attempt to further examine what was happening to me, Dr. Fin said he was signing my release from the hospital and that he would prescribe an inhaler in case the cough came back. My chest was hurting, and I did not feel well so naturally I disagreed with his professional opinion and gave him a side-eye of disapproval as I looked over the untested urine sample sitting on the counter. Dr. Fin had been going through the motions of compliance and perhaps even missed a few steps. Perhaps he was too busy with the only other two patients in the emergency room, or perhaps he truly didn't know what the issue was with me, perhaps he was tired, perhaps he didn't care, perhaps he thought I was exaggerating, or perhaps he was just following his compliance protocols. Ultimately Dr. Fin gave me a prescription for an inhaler that did not solve my issue and recommended that I go see an internal medicine doctor. Dr. Fin was operating (pun intended) from a place of compliance, and it made me feel disregarded, uncared for, and ultimately didn't help me resolve the medical issue I was facing.

Instead of going to the beach, we moved up our flight and ended our South Beach trip a little early. As we were transitioning back home, I managed to keep my symptoms at bay (another pun for you my dear educators) with over-the-counter medicine, cough drops, and occasional pumps of the inhaler. I had tried to call an internal medicine doctor as Dr. Fin had recommended, but all available appointments were several weeks out. I figured that by the time I would see an internal medicine doctor, my cough would probably be gone, but I scheduled a doctor's visit a month out anyway. The night I made it back to my home, I started violently coughing again. This time it was around 3 a.m. when the coughing started, and I was really afraid because not only was it difficult to breathe, but now my chest was really hurting. My mom was not there to subtly encourage me to go to the emergency room again, so I woke up and made some tea and took some more cough syrup. I started googling my symptoms, and an ad popped up for a medical scheduler. Since it was 3 a.m., my thinking was pretty cloudy, and I can't exactly remember what in my research led me to download the medical scheduler app, but I am so thankful that I did. I found an opening with an internal medicine doctor the very next day on the app and was a little doubtful that the appointment was legitimate since I had never heard of the app. When I arrived at the doctor's office, the appointment was, in fact, legitimate, and I met Dr. Marlin.

Dr. Marlin is an internal medicine doctor, and with her gentle eyes, she welcomed me to share with her what was going on and what had brought me in to see her. I started to explain to her what had happened in Miami, and she began to take copious notes. Something didn't make sense to her—why would a seemingly healthy woman be having difficulty breathing. The doctor's appointment was scheduled for 15 minutes, but Dr. Marlin was determined to figure out what was going on with me. After about two hours of asking me questions, doing some lab work, running some tests, and also requesting that I go get X-rays of my chest, Dr. Marlin made it clear that whatever was ailing me would be found. She told me that some of my lab work would take a couple of days, but in the meantime, the labs that she had run showed that I had an obstruction and that she would need to take a closer look at them once the X-rays came back, but that she would prescribe pills to control my cough attacks. She felt certain that she had a strong idea of what was ailing me but wanted to wait until my lab work returned to make a complete diagnosis. The prescription pills started working pretty quickly, and the next few days that I was waiting for the labs, I had very little coughing. When the labs came back, Dr. Marlin's office staff called and asked me to come back to the doctor's office so that she could go over the results. I was a little nervous and feared the worst possible results. But thankfully the reason she wanted me to go back to see her was because she said that she had seen how afraid I was and also how upset I had been that I had felt the prior doctor had dismissed my symptoms and not properly cared for me. Dr. Marlin's thorough investigation, questioning, and lab work found that my system was being attacked by a parasite and that because of my weekend immune system, I had caught an acute case of bronchitis and was suffering from asthma-like symptoms. She also found that I was extremely vitamin D and iron deficient. Dr. Marlin, perhaps, went through her compliance protocols to identify what was ailing me, but the way she treated me was with dignity and respect. Dr. Marlin showed up as a true medical professional and not only did she do her job as a doctor, but she treated me as a human being and cared for my humanity. Her treatment toward me made me feel cared for and that together we were going to find a solution to what was happening with me. I've never been so motivated to follow doctor's orders, but I took my medication faithfully as now I was invested in my health even more because of the level of investment she had also made in making me healthy again.

Classrooms and medical offices are not that different, and neither are educators and doctors. Well, the pay and respect you receive, that is different, and as I stated before, we definitely need to change that. But the idea of understanding context beyond compliance to having a larger impact can easily be applied to both fields. In the case of Dr. Fin and Dr. Marlin, there was a tremendous difference in how each approached their work to understand context. As medical professionals, I am sure they both had a protocol they had to comply with, but what made the difference in their compliance was their personal approach in understanding context. As you can imagine from the description of the scenarios, Dr. Fin was dry and direct. He made assumptions without a thorough inquiry process and ultimately really did very little for my healing. On the other hand, Dr. Marlin was kind and compassionate and took time to deeply understand my context and what was happening in my life to bring me to that point. The night I went to the hospital, the emergency room was not busy, and Dr. Fin could have taken the time to better understand my context even if he wasn't an internal medicine doctor, but he chose compliance and missed out on an opportunity to connect with me, but more importantly, he missed the opportunity to deeply understand my context to help me heal.

Principle 2: Understand Context Beyond Compliance

The second principle is *Understand Context Beyond Compliance*. What we believe about children and what they are capable of achieving may be tainted by things like compliance labels that can create a narrative about where they come from and negatively affect our belief in where they are going. Or worse yet, not understanding a student's context can have a detrimental impact on their life. Ultimately, both Dr. Fin and Dr. Marlin are doctors and their role is to identify what ails their patients and make professional recommendations on how they can be cured. Similarly, whether you are a master teacher, a music teacher, or a beginning teacher, your role as an educator is to educate. Just like it was critical for Dr. Marlin to gather insights in my medical history, it is, in fact, important to understand the current context of a student's life and understand what compliance labels like "at-risk," "low socioeconomic status," and "special education" really mean. And regardless of the context or the compliance labels, an educator's role is to educate, just as a doctor's role is to heal. And just like Dr. Marlin, if you embrace the second principle and understand context beyond compliance, you can make a difference in the education you provide to children, and sometimes this can be the spark a student needs to care more about their education because you showed a deep level of care.

Every year, thanks to the policies our policymakers enact during legislative sessions, schools have a compliance checklist they must go through to receive funding and support to educate our children. I get it. As a prior administrator, I know, even though there is funding tied to some of the compulsory things that have to be done, it doesn't make them right or even fruitful to support the academic development of children. For example, our education system has required us to use deficit labels to identify the needs of children and get additional funding, but there isn't a policy that regulates or mandates what we speak or believe about children, their families, or the communities they live in. At the core, the second principle boils down to being human and understanding where your student is coming from. What are their lived experiences, what is going on in their lives right now that may impact their ability to learn in your classroom, what supports do they need to show up as their most authentic selves and enjoy the learning process in your classroom.

I was born in the United States of America. I am the daughter of a Cuban political asylum–seeking father and once undocumented Mexican[1] mother whose common hope was a better future for their children. I often identify myself as a CubAMex because of my rich multicultural identity, although legal forms asking for your identity are never that inclusive. My father left our family when I was about to turn five years old and my mom was eight months pregnant with my little sister. My mom had to start working full time while simultaneously trying to learn English since, until then, she had depended on my father for everything. I was growing up in one of Austin's highest crime rate zip codes and attending some of Austin's less resourced Title I[2] schools. Our small community was often in the news because of gang violence, drugs, and prostitution rings. During this chapter of my childhood, I experienced hunger, trauma, sadness, abandonment, and shame as well as support, laughter, joy, happiness, and love. Going to school was one of the highlights that I would look forward to.

The majority of people living in my community were like my mother, undocumented and low-income, but also like my mother, many were very hard-working. They were probably the parents educators often labeled as ones who don't care because they didn't come to parent-teacher conferences or family nights or other school events; my mom was certainly one of those. She was too busy working three jobs to put food on the table, trying to learn English at night to earn more money and work less, spend as much quality time as she could squeeze in with us, and just flat out was intimidated by a system that she didn't know how to navigate through.

Inside our small apartment, we had all the essentials. We had mostly working appliances, a decent living room set, a dining table, beds in each of the rooms with a mismatch of sheets, and an assortment of hand-me-down clothes from my cousins or clothes purchased from Goodwill, garage sales, or the occasional trips to Wal-Mart. We had food in our refrigerator and freezer—although a lot of it with bright orange WIC[3] labels, and oftentimes off-brand cereal bags with no toys or puzzles. And we had a lot of spinach—my mom seemed to be obsessed with how strong and healthy Popeye the Sailor Man (yeah, the cartoon) was and she made us eat each spinach often. We also had a few toys—also mostly hand-me-downs or ones we had purchased from garage sales or that we made ourselves. We had very few books, mostly the ones we bought at garage sales, too.

I was labeled as an "at-risk" student. In my community, there were other students who were labeled "at-risk." But each of our "at-risk" situations was unique. For example, our family units were entirely different. Some of the kids in my neighborhood were fortunate to have both parents, some like me had a single mother, some had a parent who had been or still was incarcerated, and some had a parent who had been killed. And some didn't even know their parents and lived with a family member like an aunt, uncle, or grandparent. Each of our circumstances was different. The "at-risk" label is too broad and generalized and serves as a passive structural mechanism to categorize children for the basic benefits of funding and accountability. This is true for the other labels as well. While perhaps well-intended, the labels placed on students subconsciously send a message— that they are different, they need something, they lack, they are incomplete, they are less than, they are unworthy, they are poor, they are not good enough, and they are going to fail. I wonder what Dr. Fin saw when he was reviewing my intake chart that would subsequently result in the approach he took with me in the emergency room. I wonder what our educators think about our children when they are reviewing "student charts" for their incoming class. I had a teacher that was like Dr. Marlin who took time to understand our family context beyond compliance, and as a result of that, I believe that she changed the trajectory of my educational journey.

It was Christmas Eve, and there was a knock at our front door. Since my father had left, every time a doorbell rang I would be the first one to bolt to the door. This knock was no different. I was playing in the living room with my little sister next to the TV and the Christmas tree with a small arrangement of beautifully wrapped gifts—a skill I have yet to learn from my mama. I opened the door, and to my disappointment but to my great surprise, Mrs. Dahlia was standing outside with a couple of other teachers and each one of them had bags of gifts in both of their hands! Mrs. Dahlia looked at me and said "Merry Christmas" and asked me if my mom was available. My mom was standing right behind me with a face filled with gratitude.

Mrs. Dahlia and the other teachers had collected money and purchased gifts for my sisters and me. In a recent conversation Mrs. Dahlia had had with my mother, she had learned that not only was my mom single but that recently someone had broken into our small apartment and had stolen the money she was saving up for Christmas presents. Theft and vandalism are often a byproduct of poverty. One of the gifts I received was a forest green Coleman sleeping bag for camping—I can still see it when I close my eyes. In my life, I had never gone camping. I didn't even know what camping was, but it was such a fun gift! I remember coming back from Christmas vacation and thanking Mrs. Dahlia for the sleeping bag she had given to me. Mrs. Dahlia, of course, graciously said I was very welcome and asked what I planned to do with my gift. At first, I felt a little embarrassed as I knew she had seen the circumstances we were living in and possibly knew my secret that I had never gone camping. As the year continued and when she saw me at school, she would make it a point to ask me how I was doing, what I was learning in class, and how my mom was doing. Mrs. Dahlia never once looked down on me or spoke to me in a disrespectful manner; instead, her interactions with me were always filled with respect, dignity, and compassion. One year during my sister's parent-teacher conference, my mom confided in Mrs. Dahlia some of the challenges she was facing with me. Not only did I seem to not be engaging as much in my learning, but I was also becoming a little disrespectful at home. And after that, every time I saw Mrs. Dahlia, her check-ins became even more personable. She began to ask me about the future and if I knew how to accomplish my goals. Even though she was my younger sister's teacher, I felt like she was my teacher. She continued to make me feel like she deeply cared about me and understood some of the barriers I was facing to reach my dreams. I vividly remember that one day I had somehow revealed to her that I wanted to be a mariachi singer—something that I had seen my father be very passionate about before he left. Mrs. Dahlia was organizing that year's Cinco de Mayo festival and approached me one day and said she wanted me to be the closing performance—she wanted me to sing a famous mariachi song. I confided in her that I couldn't because I felt like I couldn't sing and that I was too fat to get on stage. She chuckled at my responses and said that she'd have a solution for me the next day. I went home that night wondering what kind of solution she was talking about. The next day she came to school and pulled me aside and told me, when I truly wanted something, I had to work for it. She made it a point to tell me that life has a way of placing barriers to reaching your dreams but that each person has a way to overcome them. She told me that if I perceived that being fat was what was keeping me from being on stage, then the solution was to work out and get healthier. I didn't end up losing weight at the time nor singing in that year's Cinco de Mayo performance, but her life lesson has stayed with me until this very day. Mrs. Dahlia is an example of what happens when, as an educator, you take time to understand context beyond compliance. Because of the way she treated me in that season of my life, I resolved that teachers were part of my team and that I could count on them because they really cared.

As I shared in the first chapter, educators have a very special position in the lives of children. When they are operating with compassion and empathy and are really grounded in their why, the second principle, understanding context beyond compliance, becomes easier. I know the last few years of COVID have caused massive strain on an already overworked, underpaid, and certainly underappreciated group of human beings who invest their time and talent into developing our next generation—however, my personal plea, as the previous "at-risk student" who is on the other side, is to take care of yourself, my dear educators, so that you can boldly walk in your purpose and use your talent to have generational impact in the lives of children. To have a real impact, you have to have a real understanding of what is going on the life of a student.

Another great example of an amazing teacher who connected beyond context was my fourth grade teacher Mrs. Peony. Every morning, Mrs. Peony would greet each one of us with such kindness as we walked into her classroom, even my classmate Sammy, who was one of the most rambunctious kids in our school. Mrs. Peony always took time to connect with each of us and ask us how we were doing and what was something new that we had learned that we were excited about. I loved her class, especially math. But, I especially remember one day where we had taken a big step from numerical expressions to word problems. During class, the math lesson had seemed so straightforward; as a class we had read the math problem and had created the formulas that we needed to solve it.

I was so excited to do my homework that I had decided to get a head start on the bus. But what I quickly realized was that word expressions were much more difficult than I thought. English is my second language, and when I was reading the problems, all the words were jumbled in my head and nothing made sense. I couldn't seem to easily extract the numbers from the narrative.

I got home extremely exasperated, and my mom was unable to help me because she didn't speak English. Luckily my mom was resourceful and found me support—I'll tell you more about that in a later chapter. The next day Mrs. Peony asked for volunteers to put the answers on the board. When only a few people raised their hands she called on me to put my answer on the board. I was usually the first to volunteer, but I felt a little guilty because the night before I had been unable to complete my homework on my own. I walked to the board begrudgingly, and Mrs. Peony congratulated me for my correct answer. During recess that day, she pulled me aside to ask me what was wrong. She had noticed that I hadn't been my chirpy self that jumped out of the seat to volunteer. With hesitation and fear that I might get in trouble, I confided in her that I had received help in doing my homework. She graciously inquired as to the reason. When I explained to her that it was because I was having trouble understanding the word problems in English, she was empathetic.

Mrs. Peony was an immigrant to this country and understood the challenges that I was facing in translating the English problems into my native tongue, then still having to process the numerical expression. Going forward in class, she made it a point to provide additional support when I needed it and or felt stuck. More importantly, she made it clear that knowing two languages was an asset. In class one day, she asked who could solve problems in other languages, and I proudly raised my hand. Mrs. Peony made it a point to build a meaningful relationship with each one of her students, and as a result, I felt safe in asking for help.

Mrs. Peony understood my circumstances, but she did not let that become an excuse for holding low expectations for me. On the contrary, she built a meaningful relationship with me— that of an educator to a student, which is the third principle we will cover next. Mrs. Peony wasn't my best friend, she wasn't my parent, nor my therapist, Mrs. Peony was my educator. She understood and acknowledged the challenges I was facing and provided the additional support I required to learn the content without "dumbing it down" or lowering the bar. The second principle to help unlock your key to a deeper connection is to *Understand Context Beyond Compliance*.

Five Practices to Understand Context Beyond Compliance

Understanding context beyond compliance can be a daunting task because it requires you to attempt to understand the world of another through their lens while checking in with your own biases and, at the same time, showing up to do your absolute best work. It makes me think of the time I served as a waitress and had a platter full of plates and a wine glass on the edge—a very delicate balance. But one that we must do, especially if we want to have a deeper connection with our students. Additionally as I shared in the introduction, our development is shaped through the people and experiences that we go through in life, and thus, it is highly possible that your students will have different backgrounds than you, not wrong, just different. What I believe is important to embrace, is that no one had the opportunity to choose the circumstances they were born into, but it is our responsibility to work together to make this better place for all. Next are five practices that educators used with me and/or I have seen great educators in the field use to apply Principle 2: Understand Context Beyond Compliance.

1. **Build trusting relationships**: Hands down, the best strategy to understand context beyond compliance is to take the time to build authentic relationships with your students and get to know them on a more personal level where they trust you and you trust them. This can be done with one-on-one conversations, class projects, show-and-tell activities, and student highlights. Showing genuine interest in the life, experiences, and challenges a student is facing will give you a better understanding of who they are as well as create a stronger bond with them. Remember what the late veteran educator Rita Pierson[4] said in her viral video, "Every kid needs a champion," "Kids don't learn from people they don't like." Create a safe and inclusive classroom environment where students feel comfortable sharing their thoughts, ideas, and concerns. Additionally, when you interact with students, ensure that you are coming from a place of humble inquiry (Schein)[5] to learn more about them and where they come from.

2. **Listen actively**: Listen actively to your students when they speak, not just to their words, but also to their emotions, body language, and nonverbal cues. This can help you understand their perspectives, motivations, and emotions, which may not be apparent through

compliance labels or academic performance. Notice and wonder about the difference and similarities between your students and find creative ways to gain insight into those differences.

3. **Educate yourself about labels**: Educate yourself about the diversity of students' contexts by learning about cultural responsiveness, trauma-informed practices, and other relevant topics like the labels we use to identify students. To be clear, I am not a proponent of these labels, but as long as they exist, they can guide you to the general vicinity of a student's context. For example, an English-language learner doesn't always speak Spanish, and if they do, they aren't always Mexican. By investing time to gain a more nuanced and holistic understanding of your students' contexts, you will support your practice to move beyond compliance labels and foster a supportive and inclusive learning environment that promotes student success.

4. **Embed context into curriculum**: Recognize that each student has a unique context, which may include their cultural background, socioeconomic status, family dynamics, personal interests, and learning style. Crosswalk your scope and sequence with activities that may allow you to foster a dialogue about different contexts and allow the students to lead the conversation. Avoid making assumptions or generalizations based on compliance labels, and strive to understand each student's context from a strengths-based perspective and from their lived experience. For example, let's say that the majority of students are first-generation students with parents and families who build or clean homes. During a math lesson, create an activity lifting up that contractors like construction workers or domestic home cleaners are entrepreneurs and use their business savvy to acquire new contracts to fuel the lesson. There is literally math, science, reading, and art in almost everything, and what I learned from master educators is the ability to make curriculum relevant.

5. **Understand your students' community:** Oftentimes, because of varying reasons, educators do not live in the same community as their students. Take the time to truly understand the community where your students come from. Research the history, demographics, and cultural nuances of the community. Visit local libraries, parks, restaurants, gyms, and other places where students spend their time outside of the classroom. By gaining a deeper understanding of the community, you can better connect with your students and recognize the context in which they live, learn, and grow. And, trust me, when you run into a student at a local store, it's like you are a movie star. They are so proud to show you off to their family!

Novela Feature Case Study: Educators Understanding Context Beyond Compliance to Decrease Chronic Absenteeism

Background: Ms. Rose teaches at a Title 1[6] school in a small city. Recently she noticed that one of her students, Estrella, was either very late to class or missed class all together. But when she did come to class, Estrella was always fighting with her classmates and being disruptive. As it stood, Ms. Rose was already having a very difficult year because of her move from a large urban district to a small city and wished that she could figure out what was going on with Estrella. When Ms. Rose worked at a large urban district, even though they had thousands of students, they had created a way of knowing what was going on with each student and worked together to support them holistically. But in this school district, it seemed like everything was very compliance-driven. Ms. Rose tried to speak with Estrella on several occasions, but she would ultimately just brush her off and tell her just to mark her with another tardy or absence.

Challenge: Ms. Rose didn't know what to do because she knew that if Estrella missed one more class, she was going to have to sign paperwork with the school so that she and her family could have a truancy court appointment to determine the reason for her absences. A terrible policy, but one that she knew that she would have to comply with. Ms. Rose went to the office to ask if they knew anything about why Estrella was missing so much school. Marisol at the front office shared that she didn't know much because every time she called the number they had listed, the line was out of service. Marisol shared that Thursdays Estrella's mom would usually pick her up from the school with two of her other siblings.

Application of Principle 2:

Ms. Rose noticed on Estrella's enrollment paperwork that she was labeled "at-risk," "low socioeconomic status," and "English-language learner." Great, that doesn't tell me much, she thought. Ms. Rose resolved that on Thursday, she would wait for Estrella's mom to learn more about what was going on. When the school day ended, Ms. Rose hurried to the pickup line in hopes to catch Estrella's mom. As she was nearing the pickup area, she was grateful that Estrella was still there. Estrella and Ms. Rose waited for almost two hours for her mom to come to school.

"Is she usually late?" Ms. Rose finally asked.

"Yeah. But I told you that you don't have to wait," Estrella exclaimed.

"I want to," Ms. Rose replied.

"Why?" Estrella asked.

"Because you have missed a lot of school, and I don't want you to get in big trouble," Ms. Rose shared.

"I won't get in trouble if you stop reporting my tardies and absences," Estrella replied sarcastically.

"Well, I can't do that. Estrella. And every time I ask you what is going on you won't tell me so I am hoping to speak with your mom so I can understand what is going on," Ms. Rose said.

"She knows," Estrella said softly while looking down to the ground.

"She knows?" Ms. Rose repeated. "What do you mean she knows? How can she let you miss so much school?"

"It's not like she wants to Ms. Rose. And it's not like I want to miss school either. I just have to," Estrella said not wanting to engage in the conversation further.

"If you don't want to and she doesn't want you to, then why do you do it?" Ms. Rose pushed gently.

"Because my father recently went to jail and my mom didn't have any money and now has to have multiple jobs so she can feed us. And sometimes there isn't anyone she can leave my little brothers with if the señora who takes care of them is unavailable, so I have to stay home and watch them," Estrella replied with a tinge of embarrassment.

"Oh, Estrella, I am so sorry. I didn't know. Why didn't you tell me every time I asked you?" Ms. Rose replied.

"You mean tell my business in front of the entire classroom so they can make fun of me? As it is, everyone always laughs at me when I speak English because of my accent," Estrella rebutted.

"That's fair. I apologize for not creating space to have these conversations in private with you. When your mom gets here, let's set up a time so we can figure out how the school can support you and her during this very difficult time," said Ms. Rose as she stood next to Estrella to wait for her mom.

Impact on Students:

Understanding Individual Needs and Interests:
By understanding what was going on in Estrella's life, Ms. Rose was able to better understand what needs she had as

a learner. Taking time to understand some of the challenges Estrella was facing allowed Ms. Rose to build a relationship with her and gain insight into areas that she may work with the school to offer additional support. One of the best possible ways to leverage the labels placed on students is by taking time to understand individual needs that often go beyond the classroom.

Meaningful and Relevant Learning Experiences:
While Ms. Rose understood that she was teaching in a different community, she wanted to ensure that she made her teaching meaningful and relevant to her students. After the interaction with Estrella, Ms. Rose took time to better understand where students where coming from and what interests they had and curated the curriculum to ensure she was creating a rich learning experience. Additionally, when appropriate, she used news stories and world events to engage her students in the learning journey.

Differentiation and Inclusivity:
Ms. Rose created a deeper connection with each of her students so they could feel supported and empowered in their learning journey. She didn't want another issue like the one Estrella and her mom were facing to sneak up on her and was determined to create an environment that addressed all of her students' learning needs and styles. She made an effort to differentiate her instruction and assignments to accommodate the diverse needs of her students.

Summary

In this case study, Ms. Rose, a teacher at a Title 1 school, goes beyond compliance to understand the context of Estrella's chronic absenteeism. By patiently waiting to speak with Estrella's mother, Ms. Rose uncovers the challenging circumstances Estrella faces, including her father's incarceration and her mother's multiple jobs. This knowledge allows Ms. Rose to build a meaningful connection with Estrella, tailor her teaching to meet individual needs, and create a supportive and inclusive learning environment for all her students. By understanding context beyond compliance, Ms. Rose addresses chronic absenteeism and fosters academic success by ensuring every student feels seen, heard, and supported in their educational journey.

Reflection Questions for Chapter 2—Principle 2: Understand Context Beyond Compliance

1. Reflecting on your own childhood, were any labels placed on you? If so, what were they, and how did they make you feel when you heard about them? How do you think those labels impacted your identity and sense of self?
2. Take a moment to write down all the labels that come to mind when you think about your students. Set a timer for one minute and jot down every label that comes to your mind through a stream of consciousness. What did you notice about the labels that you associate with your students?
3. As an educator, if you work with students who have labels placed on them, what stories do you find yourself sharing with your friends and family about your students? What stories do they share with you? Reflect on the narratives and assumptions that may arise when discussing your students with others and how these stories may shape your perceptions and interactions with your students.
4. What actions can you take to go beyond compliance and ensure that you are valuing and acknowledging students' diverse backgrounds, identities, beliefs, and cultures and creating an inclusive and respectful learning environment where students feel seen, heard, and valued?

Notes

1   I won't go into the details of geo-political immigration reforms and policies, but to readers who are wondering, my family's immigration from my mother's side was a direct result of my grandfather serving in the U.S. and Mexico Bracero program in 1942.

2   https://www.kut.org/austin/2016-02-05/restoring-a-neighborhood-a-street-at-a-time

3   WIC means the Special Supplemental Nutrition Program for Women, Infants and Children authorized by section 17 of the Child Nutrition Act of 1966, 42 U.S.C. 1786.

4   https://www.ted.com/talks/rita_pierson_every_kid_needs_a_champion?language=en

5   https://www.goodreads.com/en/book/show/17381706

6   Title I schools are given additional funding: from website "provides financial assistance to local educational agencies (LEAs) and schools with high numbers or high percentages of children from low-income families to help ensure that all children meet challenging state academic standards." https://www2.ed.gov/programs/titleiparta/index.html

3

Principle 3: Foster Meaningful Interactions

One day while visiting my stepfather's family in Cienfuegos, Cuba, my sister and I decided to go sit outside with one of my cousins at the *malecon* to enjoy the breeze and just hang out. We didn't really have a lot of things to say to my cousin because we rarely talked to her due to the cost associated with making phone calls and usually calls were reserved for the adults. So while sitting by the *malecon*, we were just making small talk with my cousin and letting the time pass by. Then one of her friends, Danny, who was out for a bike ride saw us and rode toward where we were all sitting. Danny greeted us with an immense smile from ear to ear and asked us where we were visiting from. After a few moments of polite introductions, Danny blurted out a request for us to share funny stories or jokes with him. I was confused at his request, and my perplexed look made him chuckle. He asked again and then I said that I didn't have any funny stories or jokes that I could think of. He was shocked and said, "You mean to tell me you come from one of the world's richest countries, a country where so many people want to live, and you don't have any jokes or stories to share?" He chuckled again and started sharing jokes and stories with us. Before long we were all engrossed in exchanging stories, making up jokes, and telling more about each other's lives as the evening started to settle in. We had literally begun as strangers, but with

DOI: 10.4324/9781003401018-4

Danny's infectious joy and indirect push to build a relationship through storytelling and jokes, we became friends in an
afternoon. Not only did we learn a lot from Danny, but we also
learned a lot of things from my cousin. It was an unforgettable
experience, and I feel so grateful for the lesson Danny taught
me that afternoon.

A few years after visiting Cuba, I had the opportunity to
move to my mother's home country, Mexico. I moved to a city
that I wasn't familiar with and a neighborhood where I didn't
know anyone. One day as I was still unpacking boxes, I heard
someone clinking the gate of my home and came out to see who
it was. It was my neighbor Paulina, who I had greeted the other
day when I was moving things from my car into the house.

"How's the moving?" Paulina asked.

"It's going, but I still have a lot to do," I replied.

"Well if you need anything at all, don't hesitate to reach out.
Here is my number in case I am not home," she kindly shared.

"Thank you," I replied and went inside to continue packing.

A few more days passed, and I was baking some cupcakes
and getting ready to watch a show on television when I heard
the clinking sound at my gate again. I wasn't expecting visitors
and didn't really know anyone, so at first I thought I would just
ignore the sound. But the clinking sound continued, so I peeked
through the window and, to my surprise, Paulina was standing
outside. I opened the door and greeted her.

"Good afternoon, Paulina."

"Good afternoon, Marcela," she smiled at me.

"How are you?" I asked trying see what she needed without
directly asking her if she needed something.

"I'm doing well. It's such a beautiful day, and I just came
back from taking a walk in the park and running errands."

"That's nice. It looks like it is a beautiful day to be out and
about."

"Yes, sometimes I go with some of the other neighbors to a
dance class, but it seemed too nice today to be inside. Maybe next
time you can join me for a walk?"

"Yes, that would be nice. I would like that." Still unsure of
what she had been clinking my gate for, I started to tell her that

I hope she enjoyed the rest of her day when she interrupted me and asked if I liked coffee.

"Yeah, I love coffee and drink it all the time. I was actually going to drink a cup now with some cupcakes I am baking."

"Yummy, that sounds amazing. I was thinking about drinking a cup of coffee this afternoon, too, but drinking coffee with a cupcake sounds much better."

Darn, I set myself up for this one.

"Well, if you'd like, you could come in and enjoy a cup of coffee with me and taste the cupcakes I made."

Paulina's eyes lit up, and she quickly accepted my invitation.

The next three hours felt never-ending. Paulina told me stories about her children, about her life, about the neighbors, about everything. Her approach to storytelling was quite entertaining as she would open with a story and then something would make her think of another story and then another and then she would make her way back to closing each story she began telling.

After Paulina left, I felt a little flustered that I had "wasted" time in spending my afternoon just listening to her stories, drinking coffee, and eating cupcakes. I initially thought I had more productive and important things to do.

Then as my time in Mexico would continue, I realized that I really enjoyed when Paulina would come over and we would share coffee with stories and some kind of treat. Throughout my time there, I built a relationship with Paulina by spending time with her and sharing stories with one another. When I moved back to the US, I was hit with a wave of sadness in the first few months because I realized what I had experienced in Mexico and a little bit in Cuba was actually something very precious. The time we spend with one another to tell stories is not aligned with capitalism but most definitely aligns with our shared humanity. As a person, I felt better connected to Danny and Paulina and others whom I take time to build relationships with. But building relationships with others is hard and takes an investment of time, especially students. Think about the story I shared about Jose; I didn't do a good job with building a relationship with him. I was focused on my teaching and my classroom outcomes and was frustrated that I couldn't teach Jose the curriculum because of his outbursts in class. Educators should provide support to tend to the individual needs and differences of children. I should have adjusted my classroom management so that I could meet the needs of Jose and invite him to actively participate in his learning. If I would have invested the time into building a relationship with him in meaningful ways instead of sending him to the office, our interactions would have led me to a better understanding of his needs as a learner.

Principle 3: Foster Meaningful Interactions

Wearing a shoe that doesn't fit is terribly uncomfortable. Yet every day in schools, children step into classrooms wearing shoes that don't fit, both literally and figuratively. It is truly a gift to be able to show up as your most authentic self in every space you enter. The third principle is *Foster Meaningful Interactions*.

In classrooms across the country, it comes naturally and easily for some students and teachers to show up in spaces as their complete selves as if they already know each other's stories because, perhaps, they share a common identity, like their racial background. But what happens when a student and teacher don't share a common identity and their demographics are, perhaps, polar opposites? What happens when there is a difference in things like language, beliefs, identity, values, books, and food. Without building a relationship with students, it could feel like figuratively putting on a shoe that doesn't fit. Students may hide part of their identity to assimilate, pronounce their name with a different enunciation or completely change it so others won't struggle, eat food that may be too bland or not include comfort staples they would eat at home, wear clothing that looks similar to what is on TV, or code switch to share a narrative of their identity that assimilates to a dominant culture like watching pop culture TV and talking about it. This was certainly my case, but I am grateful for the educators who were like Danny and Paulina and found a way to build a relationship with me.

In seventh grade, there was a lot going on in my life. My mother had just remarried and informed us that we would be moving to an entirely different community. I felt like I would be stripped away from my friends and the comfort of my daily routine, and I wished with all of my seventh-grade heart that we could just stay in the community we were in. Why did her getting remarried mean we had to leave? Why couldn't my new stepdad just move into our apartment?

Since sixth grade, I had been riding the city bus to school and walking a few blocks with my classmates in Austin. In seventh grade, my friends and I started getting much closer. We started wearing the same baggy pants with oversized T-shirts and styling our hair the same way, and we would tell one another that we were family. Growing up in a neighborhood that was riddled with gangs, I knew better not to get involved with any gang, but somehow in my community, you still had to be part of something even if it was unspoken. My mom would warn me repeatedly not to keep company with anyone that resembled a gang member and was relatively strict with when and with whom my sisters and I would go outside. Usually, the only times we played outside were on the weekend when someone from our family or a trusted neighbor could be outside with us and supervise that nothing would happen. So, for me, it was a real treat to ride the city bus without my mom and all my neighbors constantly watching over me.

I will never forget one day that my mom had to leave early for work so I decided to change up my look and wear makeup that I wasn't allowed to wear. I went into my mom's makeup bag and grabbed her lipstick, mascara, and eyeliner. The trend was to wear really dark maroon lips, but my mom didn't have that color so I used her eyeliner to shape my lips like I had seen the other girls do and filled it in with the red lipstick. The red lipstick and black liner made the perfect shade of a dark maroon color and I was so excited to show off my new dark lips to my friends. As we got off the bus, it was almost as if my new lipstick invited more trust with my friends. As we approached the school, I saw my best friend Roman, and he nervously came up to me and said that he needed to speak with me. Roman told me that he was holding a little bit of weed for his cousin Joel, who was in high school, and that Joel would come by and pick it up after school that day. Roman said that because he was a guy, he was probably going to look suspicious so asked me if I would be willing to hold his backpack until Joel got to the school. I knew better not to do drugs, but at the time, I didn't see a problem just carrying Roman's backpack to avoid him getting in trouble. When we got to school, Roman went with the guys to the back part of the school and I went my way to the front of the school to hang out with all of my girlfriends. I was keeping an eye out for Roman to see where he would leave his backpack so I could go pick it up when I heard my friends saying my mom was here. I was so confused, whose mom? Certainly not mine because I had made sure my mom went to work before I took her makeup. And since she worked multiple jobs, I had a plan to make sure to remove it before she got home.

As I was letting it sink in what they were saying to me, I felt a hard yank to my hair.

The pull of my hair came so fast that immediately I was in shock and speechless to see my mom standing in front of me. My friends were right—it was my mom. When I looked toward her, I was so ashamed to even look her in the eyes. My mom was beyond disappointed; she was looking at her daughter who left her home wearing one thing and now looked totally different. She had no words for me other than get my backpack because we were going home. The only thing I could think about at that moment was Roman. I wasn't going to be there for him to carry his backpack, and my hope was that he wouldn't get in trouble. My mom took me home, and as a consequence of my actions, my mom informed me that we would be moving up our move to Pflugerville and that over the next few days, she would be withdrawing from the school and enrolling me in my new school.

At the time, the move seemed so extreme because of the dramatic change in my environment. Everything was different. We had moved from a very small two-room apartment in a distressed neighborhood and community to a three-bedroom home in a quiet neighborhood with a large backyard surrounded by trees. In our new community, there were restaurants and not just fast-food establishments. When I went to school, everything there was different, too. The building was very nice and clean as opposed to the tattered building I had been learning in, the air was crisp and not muggy, and everyone looked and dressed differently.

One of my favorite desserts is *arroz con leche*. My grandma's recipe calls for the *arroz* to simmer with small pieces of cinnamon sticks. When I moved to the small town of Pflugerville, I felt like a cinnamon stick inside a pot of rice. There were a handful of other students who also looked like me, but we were few. Although I had finished fifth grade with very high marks and was identified as gifted and talented, in sixth grade I started not engaging with my learning as much, and in seventh grade, my grades had totally started to plummet, even Spanish class, which is my first language. When we moved to Pflugerville, my grades were getting even worse. As an act of rebellion for stripping me from my friends and school, I would purposefully not turn in any of my homework and would make it a daily effort to be late. I would talk to Roman over the phone daily and share with him how much I missed him and our friends. Roman had shared with me that he hadn't gotten caught that day that I left school, but a couple of weeks later, he was suspended because they had found weed on him. I was sad for my friend Roman and wished I was there with him and my other friends. I was struggling to make new friends in my new school. I was determined to not let this new environment affect me and was doing what I could to make my mother move us back.

One day, my new seventh-grade math teacher Ms. Sunflower asked me to come to her classroom during the lunch break. I had never seen a teacher with red hair and freckles and was a little surprised that she had approached me and asked me to come to her classroom during lunch. It kind of reminded me of the time Mrs. Iris had asked me to walk with her, but this time I hadn't stolen the classroom snail. Heck, I had just barely been there a few weeks.

During lunch, Ms. Sunflower asked me how I was liking my new school.

"It's fine, I guess," I replied non-emotionally.

"You've made a pretty big change moving from Austin to Pflugerville. Things must be very different for you," she probed.

"Yeah, they, for sure, are VERY different," I replied sarcastically.

"In what ways are they different?" she asked.

"I don't know," I replied again non-emotionally. "They just are, everything is different."

"Are you different?" she asked.

I was confused by her question. Was she asking me if I was different than the students in my new school? Yeah, absolutely, we were completely different. Or did she mean if I was a different person? While I was pondering her question, she must have seen the confusion through my weak poker face and elaborated on her question.

"Are you different, meaning are you still the same person you were who was living in Austin, or because you moved to Pflugerville, are you a different person?"

I saw where she was going with this. "I am the same person I was in Austin."

"Great, that is really great to hear. I am glad that you haven't changed who you are because of where you are."

This teacher, I thought, was so interesting. Why would I change who I was just because of where I was?

"I've noticed that you follow along with your eyes when I am teaching new lessons and your face doesn't seem confused, but you don't turn in any of your homework and you are not doing so well on the pop quizzes or the last test. Yet I know when a student is not understanding the lesson I am teaching, but you have been understanding everything, haven't you?" she paused.

I stayed quiet and thought, yeah, I had learned some of this before and at the pace she was moving it was super easy to take in the lessons she was teaching.

"Mar-SEH-lah," she pronounced my name in my native tongue. Most teachers would pronounce it slightly differently mar-SEL-uh with an English enunciation.

I smirked.

"What made you smile?" she asked.

"The way you pronounced my name. It's the same way I pronounce it and the same way my family and friends call me," I said.

"Isn't that the way it should be? Since you haven't changed who you are, then shouldn't you be called by your name?" she asked.

"Yeah, but I am not. Not here. Not by most of my teachers or my classmates," I said with a little bit of a bite to my tone.

"I see, well, then you are just going to have to correct them when they mispronounce it or change who you are," she said jokingly.

"Yeah, I am not changing."

"I'm glad. Don't change who you are. But you do have to make some changes."

"Like what."

"Well, you are responsible for your future. I can't imagine how hard the change was to move here, but if you continue not to do your homework, you will not have a good future." She paused and treaded lightly with her next statement.

"I can tell you are very smart and that you are not happy here, but you are going to have to make a choice to make the best of it and get a really good education or be defiant and sit in my class and the class of the other teachers and decide not to learn. At the end of your journey from middle school and then high school, you can have the future you want waiting for you or the future that you let your actions decide for you."

This lunch got really serious, I thought.

"I am here to support you every step of the way. I know change is very different, and although I don't look like you, I also don't look like the other teachers or students. My red hair has made me stand out plenty of times and it makes me special. You are special, and we are very lucky to have you at our school."

She continued, "I know it's very difficult to make new friends and settle into a new community when you first move to a new place. And I want you to know that this is your classroom, and if you like, you can come here during lunch."

I had been feeling very anxious at lunch because there were so many new people and I didn't really have any friends yet, so when she said that, it gave me a sense of relief.

"Thank you," I replied just before the bell rang.

A couple of weeks passed by, and I took up Ms. Sunflower's offer to eat in her classroom. Sometimes we would talk about my family and things that I did on the weekend, and other times we would chat about some of the things she had taught us in class. Ms. Sunflower showed genuine interest in my life and, in hindsight, spending time with her reminded me of the afternoons I would spend time with Paulina. We used the lunch time to share stories and build a relationship.

During class time, Ms. Sunflower would create projects for our class to complete group work. She made it a point to pick the groups for us almost every time and would facilitate the awkward interaction that a bunch of 11- and 12-year-olds have when working with each other for the first time. She had a small group protocol that she used so that before we started working on a project, each group member would have the opportunity to share a little bit of themselves and how they worked best. This approach to group work really helped foster a positive culture inside of our classroom because at the end of the year, at some point, we had all had a chance to work in a group with all of our classmates. This approach also made it easier for me to make new friends during class since I would have not naturally sat next to them and/or perhaps they wouldn't have selected me to be part of their group. Slowly eating my lunch inside Ms. Sunflower's class became just a memory. But because Ms. Sunflower had taken time to build a relationship with me and created a space for me to feel part of the school community, my level of engagement went up. During class, I would not only follow along with the lesson she was sharing, but I would also raise my hand often and would start turning in all of my homework and preparing for my tests. Even though outside of class time I would begin to only wave to Ms. Sunflower, I knew that by her taking time to build a relationship, it impacted how I showed up in her class and in the school as a learner.

Ms. Sunflower had seen that I was struggling to fit into a school that didn't reflect my identity or demographics, and she had also seen my academic struggle. She intentionally built a meaningful relationship with me so that I could feel part of her classroom and the larger school community. Her actions made me feel welcomed and special. My mindset changed from feeling like I was different to feeling special. Soon it wouldn't even phase me that there were so few students who looked like me and that I was living in a different community. I got so caught up in studying and focusing on my future.

Educators have a special place in the lives of children, and when they understand the position they hold and activate it to build relationships, they can, in fact, create an impact on a student's learning environment. Building meaningful relationships is a game changer inside and outside the classroom. Had Ms. Sunflower not built a relationship with me, perhaps I would have not ever truly felt part of the community I became part of. As the late 40-year educator Rita Pierson shared on her Ted Talk "Every Kid needs a Champion," "Kids don't learn from people they don't like." Building a meaningful relationship with students can have a life-long impact on their life journeys. Imagine a classroom where a teacher was grounded in her why (Principle 1) and then went a step further to deeply understand a student's life beyond compliance (Principle 2), and then built a meaningful interactions (Principle 3) with each and every student, these principles alone could be a game changer. Those three principles impact physiological safety, trust, and ultimately encourage the exchange of knowledge!

School was a place where I entered a new world and learned new things. I traveled the world through books and expanded my mind through new ideas, creative projects, classroom discussions, and, above all, teachers whose joy of teaching was so infectious. Through my academic journey, I have had amazing teachers both inside and outside of the classroom that built a meaningful relationship with me that had a tremendous impact on my academics as well as my social-emotional learning and development.

In the Ted Talk I mentioned earlier, Ms. Pierson described a scenario where she graded one of her students' papers and he had only gotten 2 of the 20 answers correct. Ms. Pierson could have easily pointed out that the student had missed 18, but she focused on elevating the 2 he had gotten correctly. She approached the interaction with her student with a growth mindset. I am willing to bet that Ms. Pierson was an educator who took time to cultivate meaningful relationships with her students and found ways to lift them up through her interactions with them.

Five Practices to Foster Meaningful Interactions

Building meaningful relationships with students is one of the key principles to create a deeper connection with students. Building relationships takes time and effort, and it's an ongoing process that requires consistent attention and care. In the era of Zoom calls, over-enrolled classrooms, and everyone on the next level of tired, how is it even possible to build a meaningful relationship with every student? It is certainly challenging and sometimes may be impossible simply because we are human beings and relationships are complex. If you have tried to build a relationship with all the students in your classroom and find that you still can't connect with some, that is okay. Don't take it personally. But leverage your colleagues at the school to ensure that every student in your classroom has a meaningful relationship with an educator. Every student deserves to be in a learning environment where they feel seen, heard, and supported to achieve their dreams.

During the writing of this book, I reached out to Mrs. Dahlia (the same teacher from elementary school who I still keep in touch with) and asked her how she did it to build such meaningful relationships with students. She confessed that it, indeed, is challenging to have that relationship with every student, in every classroom, but that her approach was to see herself in the student. Building meaningful relationships with students is perhaps the most difficult principle because it requires both student and educator to connect and there is no single right way of doing it. Additionally it takes time, and that is a commodity that we have very little of. But the reward to creating meaningful relationships with students is huge, and, I can't say this enough, it can truly be life-changing. Find a way that works for you and work hard every day to improve your own approach. Just remember, building meaningful relationships with students can support students with ensuring their shoes fit, literally and figuratively.

1. **Show genuine interest:** Demonstrate genuine interest in your students as individuals. Take the time to learn about their interests, hobbies, and personal experiences. Show

empathy and understanding toward their challenges and celebrate their successes. Make an effort to connect with each student on a personal level to build trust and rapport. Tap into my old neighbor's Paulina's energy.

2. **Practice active listening**: Actively listen to your students when they speak, without interrupting or judgment. Show that you value their thoughts and opinions by giving them your full attention. Encourage them to share their ideas, concerns, and perspectives and validate their emotions and experiences. Active listening helps students feel heard and understood, which strengthens the teacher-student relationship. Let your smile be as infectious and inviting as Danny was on the Cuban malecón.

3. **Provide opportunities for student voice and choice**: Create opportunities for students to have a voice and choice in their learning. Allow them to share their ideas, opinions, and feedback on classroom decisions and activities. Provide choices in assignments, projects, or topics of study that align with their interests and strengths. When students feel that their opinions and choices matter, they are more likely to develop a sense of ownership and engagement in their learning leverage your understanding of a student's why.

4. **Show empathy and understanding**: Practice empathy and understanding toward your students' feelings, needs, and challenges. Be patient, compassionate, and nonjudgmental in your interactions with students. Acknowledge and validate their emotions, and offer support and guidance when needed. When students feel understood and supported, they are more likely to trust and connect with their teachers. Tap into Ms. Rose inspector gadget technique to really seek to understand where a student is coming from.

5. **Foster a positive classroom culture**: Create a positive classroom culture that promotes respect, inclusivity, and kindness. Set clear expectations for behavior and treat all students with fairness and equity. Encourage collaboration, mutual respect, and peer support among students.

Celebrate diversity and create an inclusive environment where all students feel valued and respected. A positive classroom culture helps students feel safe, supported, and connected, which strengthens the teacher-student relationship. Be like Ms. Sunflower and create classroom communities by curating connections among students.

Novela Feature Case Study: Physical Education Teacher Fosters Meaningful Interactions to Develop a Deeper Connection With Students

Background: Mr. Gentian taught physical education to 400 bright-eyed and very active elementary students. His daily schedule was packed from morning until the end of the day with eight different PE classes. The elementary school shared a common gym with the middle school. Often he would hang out at the gym throwing hoops so he would let the traffic die down for his way home from school. One day Mr. Gentian noticed that there were three middle school boys who were in the gym unattended. When he tried to get their attention, the boys quickly ran away but not before Mr. Gentian managed to notice that one of the boys was the older brother to one of his students. The next day he saw the middle school principal, Ms. Geranium, and made mention of the three boys in the gym unattended.

Challenge: Ms. Geranium commented that she wasn't surprised and was able to quickly identify who the other two boys were. She told him, "Don't worry, Mr. Gentian, I will talk to the students and give them a consequence for not following the rules." While Mr. Gentian knew sharing with Ms. Geranium was the right thing, his intention was never to get the boys punished.

Application of Principle 3:

"Hey Ms. Geranium, it seems like the three boys often do things like this, right?" Mr. Gentian asked.

"Yes, I can't ever seem to keep them out of my office, detention, or, in some cases, suspension," Ms. Geranium replied a bit annoyed. "I honestly don't know what to do anymore with them and their teachers are really struggling with them too," she continued.

Mr. Gentian smiled as he replied, "They really remind me of my friends and me. We were always getting into trouble and sometimes even challenged one another to see who could get in more trouble. This one year, in eighth grade, well, never mind, the point is that I know where these boys are coming from. They are looking for attention, and they just need to receive meaningful interaction."

"Between myself, our assistant principal, and most of their teachers we've interacted with them plenty of times," she continued.

"How about we try something? Since I am here every day after school just shooting hoops, why don't we invite them to form part of a club where they get to hang out with me and shoot hoops and I get the opportunity to interact with them every day and learn more about what's going on. Plus it will give me an opportunity to practice since I'll be teaching middle school next year," Mr. Gentian offered.

Over the next few months, Mr. Gentian met with the three boys after school. During the time they would spend shooting hoops, Mr. Gentian was able to learn more about each of the students. They all had complex situations happening at home, but what he learned from working with them are the same lessons he took to apply to his classroom the next year when he became a middle school teacher.

Impact on Students:

Students Built a Trusting and Respectful Relationship With an Educator:
Mr. Gentian knows that trust and respect are the foundation for meaningful relationships with students. And when

he first started working with the students, he knew that building a relationship based on trust and respect was the only way the students would stay engaged and be willing to stay after school and shoot hoops with him. During their time together, he consistently demonstrated respect toward the students by listening to their opinions, valuing their perspectives, and treating them with kindness and fairness. He also held them to high expectations and would ask them about their behavior and academic performance and, when he had the opportunity, would provide them with support and guidance to help them meet these expectations.

Students Felt Treated as Individuals:

Mr. Gentian took the time to get to know the students as individuals and understood that building relationships requires understanding and valuing their unique interests, strengths, and challenges. After a few weeks of working with the students after school, their behavior in the classroom started to improve, and Mr. Gentian commented to them how proud he was of their new behavior. The students also started sharing with Mr. Gentian some of the cool stuff they were learning in their classes. Mr. Gentian worked to establish a rapport with the students by engaging in conversations, asking open-ended questions, and actively listening to their responses. He showed a genuine interest in their lives, hobbies, and experiences outside of school, and he used this knowledge to connect with them on a personal level. By getting to know the students as individuals, Mr. Gentian was able to build trust and establish a foundation for a deeper connection with them.

Students Received Empathy and Understanding:

Mr. Gentian recognizes that young boys are still developing their social-emotional skills, and he made an effort to show empathy and understanding toward their emotions, challenges, and struggles. When they were playing basketball after school, he created a safe space where students felt comfortable expressing their feelings and validated their emotions without judgment. Mr. Gentian also shared his own experiences and stories about when he was in middle school to relate to the students and to show that he understands and cares about their well-being. By showing empathy and understanding, Mr. Gentian built a deep connection with his students, so they feel heard, supported, and valued.

Personalizing Instruction and Feedback:
While Mr. Gentian did not offer personalized instruction while they were playing hoops, he often commented on the challenges the students shared about learning in their classrooms. Mr. Gentian made note that he would make sure to use a variety of instructional strategies and learning plans to meet the needs and interests of his students.

Summary

Mr. Gentian, a PE teacher, noticed three unsupervised middle school boys in the gym. Recognizing one as the brother of his student, he shared his concerns with the middle school principal. Instead of seeking punishment, Mr. Gentian proposed forming a club where they could shoot hoops together and interact regularly. Over time, he built a trusting relationship with the boys, learning about their backgrounds and challenges. Through empathy, respect, and personalized support, Mr. Gentian transformed their behavior and strengthened their connection, emphasizing the importance of fostering meaningful interactions with students.

Reflection Questions for Chapter 3—Principle 3: Foster Meaningful Interactions

1. How can I create a space to foster meaningful interactions with students who have a sensitive situation?
2. How can I actively work on building meaningful relationships with my students to better understand their unique strengths, needs, and interests?
3. How can you involve students in decision-making processes and give them a sense of ownership in their own education so they feel valued and heard?
4. How do you collaborate with other educators or school staff to create a supportive network that promotes meaningful relationships with students? How can you leverage their expertise and support to enhance your own relationships with students?

4

Principle 4: Design High-Quality Educational Learning Environments

It was a hot summer day in Leon, Guanajuato, Mexico, and I was tired and thirsty. My family and I had driven hours to Leon to visit Zona Piel, a small maze of endless high-quality leather shoes and goods. I was in awe of both the variety and the prices offered by the shoemakers throughout the area and the goods being sold by the other vendors, including the food vendors. We walked up and down street after street looking for a few pairs of shoes that I would take home and later show off with a cute dress or outfit. We came across a store where I had found what I thought was the perfect pair of heels, but the vendor told me that he didn't have them in my size. With a little bit of disappointment, we thanked him and started to walk away. But a good business person always helps out another good business person, and he told us that just a few blocks from where we were, there was a warehouse where the shoe vendors would go buy the shoes wholesale and that they would sell to the public. He encouraged me to go there and ask for Juan and felt certain that we'd find the shoe we were looking for in the right size. Because of the layout and the

DOI: 10.4324/9781003401018-5

amount of people that visit the region, it was not customary to drive from one part of the zone to another. So we started walking to find the wholesale vendor.

If you have ever been to an outlet mall or outdoor flea market, it was like that with lanes and lanes and lanes of shoes! I was resolved to get my new shoes and decided that we would walk the "few blocks" in the scorching heat. Sometimes my sisters jab at me after I make a silly decision and say, "So, did you learn that in college?" This was definitely one of those moments. We hadn't found the warehouse, and we were all very thirsty to possibly the extent of hydration. I'm kidding, but it definitely felt that way. And just like you see in the movies that have a thirsty person looking for at least one drop of water, this nice street vendor was pushing an old two-wheel cart with large five-gallon barrels made out of glass. As he got closer, I was surprised that unlike other vendors on the street, he wasn't promoting his *agua frescas*.[1] I waved him down, and as I started walking toward him, he signaled that there was no more *agua frescas*. I couldn't believe it but, for some reason, kept walking toward him. As I approached the cart, I looked at the barrels and saw, indeed, they were all empty except for one. One barrel had a huge ice cube and at least a cup or two of the *agua fresca*.

I told the man, "Please, I see that you have at least a cup or even two in one of the barrels." He looked at the barrel and looked at me and then without saying anything proceeded to pour the cups. It was indeed enough for two cups. We took a few sips of the *agua fresca de límon*, and believe me when I tell you, it was the absolute best and most refreshing *agua fresca* I have ever had in my life.

"How much do I owe you?" I asked the man.

"Nothing," he replied. I was so confused.

I asked him again, but this time I rephrased my question in case I didn't ask correctly in Spanish. And again, he said "nothing" and to have a great day. The man started walking away, but I couldn't let it go. Why would this hard-working man gift me the *agua fresca* for free in this scorching heat. I quickly thought that perhaps he was saving it for himself, but he had a water bottle that seemed to be full of another *agua fresca*. So I was confused. When he was perhaps 20 feet away, I ran to him— okay, I jogged to him—and asked him for just another minute of his time.

"Why did you give me the *agua fresca*? I don't understand. I must pay you for what you have given to us," I said.

The man looked at me and smiled.

"I can't accept any money for what I gave you because it isn't my very best," he said. What he gave us was the watered-down version of the *agua fresca*. But I defended his watered-down *agua fresca* and said, "You don't understand—it is the best I have ever tasted."

He smiled again and said, "But it isn't my best."

Mic drop. Bruh. Or whatever cool phrases kids are using these days to describe a moment of being speechless or shocked. At most, the two cups would have cost $2, but here, in the middle of Leon, Guanajuato, this hard-working street vendor gave me a strong life lesson. Excellence. We must do things with excellence, even the smallest things.

Principle 4: Design High-Quality Educational Learning Environments

One of my all-time favorite quotes I share with folks often is, "Man's mind, stretched to a new idea, never goes back to its original dimension" (Oliver Wendall Holmes).[2] But how does this happen? How can the mind be expanded?

Education.

Designing high-quality educational learning environments (Principle 4) is the cornerstone of effective teaching. Educators made it their business to ensure I had a high-quality education, that I developed a love for learning, and that they incited and cultivated a practice of critical thinking. These life-changing educators went even beyond that—they connected with me on a much deeper human level to ensure that I understood my learning went beyond the classroom and that it happened everywhere.

Remember fifth grade? I certainly do! I had absolutely the most amazing teacher ever—okay, you are all amazing, but this teacher, Mrs. Rue, was really something special. Not only was she a Latina like me, but every day in her class, I felt deeply connected to the curriculum that was being taught. Mrs. Rue was a masterful educator that had coated the learning objectives with cultural relevance so that every student saw themselves as part of the learning experience and classroom. Additionally, she embedded activities to her classroom that centered on us as learners, much like human-centered design at the d.School at Stanford.[3] As now a former educator and a practitioner who uses human-centered and participatory design as a key approach in my work, I recognize that she used her student's interest to optimize the learning experience for me and my classmates. Mrs. Rue didn't deposit stale knowledge into our brains using the banking model that Paulo Freire refers to in his book *Pedagogy of the Oppressed*. Instead, Mrs. Rue created a welcoming and safe environment leveraging our interest and identities that led to significant learning experiences and encouraged a spirit of creativity and deep critical thinking.

Mrs. Rue knew her craft of being an educator, and she knew it well. I don't recall every single day in fifth grade, but I do recall making sure to not ever miss a class. The learning was too good and the class discussions were too much fun to miss out. During one of our social studies lessons, Mrs. Rue was giving a lesson on Texas history and how Texas was previously part of Mexico. Everyone in the classroom was shocked at this historical fact and at the edge of our seats to learn about the journey of how this all took place. The way she presented the information was like a dramatic *telenovela*, and all of my classmates and I were so engrossed in all of the classroom activities and assignments. As she went through the lesson plan, she did it in a way that lifted up the content. We were so engaged that when it was time for recess, we begged her to skip recess so we could continue the learning. She, of course, declined our request and gave our young minds a little break.

I imagine Mrs. Rue knew that the great majority of her students' families were immigrants from Latin America, and she used her cultural knowledge to bring the lesson plans to life for us and make them relevant to our fifth grade lives. Ms. Rue made it her business to ensure she knew about us and our families, and she used those insights coupled with her teaching techniques to bring the classroom learning to life. Furthermore, the way she crafted the learning experience really helped draw from the funds of knowledge (Gonzalez, et al., 2005)[4] of our families as well as helped us see our families as the leaders that they are. I'll tell you more about this approach in the next chapter, but I want to emphasize how impactful Mrs. Rue's teaching was to our learning and development.

Another experience I can clearly remember was creating a board game. A board game! As I trace back where I got some of my entrepreneurial tendencies, this experience is certainly one that stands out. Ms. Rue challenged each of her students to come up with a board game in her class. Up until that time in my life, I had a very limited notion of what a board game was. In our home, we had very few board games, and by fifth grade, I had outgrown games like Candy Land, Sorry, and Operation. First, she put us in groups with classmates that didn't sit at our table. Next, she had us talk to one another to understand what we liked and didn't like about board games. Then, she gave us a large part of the morning to brainstorm ideas and draft a prototype of our board game. When we came back from lunch that afternoon, she had colored paper, markers, glue, straws, stickers, glitter, and other crafty materials at each of our tables. Our class was so invigorated to create the board game. There was a lot of talking, laughing, and creating. My classmates and I created some really cool board games. If Mattel or other board game makers were recruiters in the room, we would have gotten million-dollar deals.

My memory of fifth grade is mostly of days filled with learning and joy. Although most of my classmates and I came from the same neighborhood and were directly impacted by poverty, the educational experience Mrs. Rue designed made me feel like we were superstars, and I looked forward to going to school every single day to learn more.

****

One of the ways I know educators LOVE their craft is their willingness to be super silly in front of their students to deliver a high-quality learning experience. As my freshman year was coming to a close, I started registering for my fall classes. Since I had taken Algebra I my freshman year, I wanted to enroll in Algebra II my first semester as a sophomore. I started asking my friends their opinion on which of the two teachers to take Alegbra II was and the consensus was to not take Ms. Orchid's class. She will fail you if she has the chance. I decided to enroll in Ms. Orchid's class despite the advice of my classmates, after all, I had improved my mathematical savvy and both numerical and written expressions were no longer a challenge for me. The first couple of weeks of classes seemed like a breeze, I felt like I had made the right choice and looked forward to attending Ms. Orchid's class. She would usually start the class in a very light-hearted way by infectiously smiling at us and repeating the same intro, "Okay kids put on your thinking caps." Her callout often reminded me of Ms. Frizzle from the Magic School Bus.[5] And then one day it was no longer fun and games, Ms. Orchid started the class with her usual intro and then quickly transitioned us into advanced concepts and the pace picked up significantly. I quickly got behind the lessons and the homework. Although she had fostered a very safe learning environment, my own complexes made it difficult for me to ask for help, so weeks went by and I kept falling further and further behind. Ms. Orchid was like an auditor, she didn't miss a beat, and one day on one of my assignments she wrote me a small note to stay after class so we could talk. I knew I hadn't stolen a snail or cheated on my homework, so I was a bit nervous to hear what she had to say. When the class bell rang, I took a little longer to gather my things discretely so that I could speak with her after class. I approached her desk hesitantly and she asked me to take a seat.

"Marcela, I have noticed that you are falling behind in my class. Is everything okay?"

"Yes, everything is fine, the lessons have just become a lot more difficult, but I am doing my best to stay caught up with all my homework." I told her.

"The issue is that the concepts keep building on each other and if there are concepts that you did not understand or are not understanding then I need to know." There was certainly no Ms. Frizzle playfulness to her tone, but rather a dedicated educator who wanted to make sure that I was understanding the content.

"Why don't we do this, go through the lessons we have covered in class and put a star next to the ones that you completely understand. During lunch or after school you can come to my class so we can review the concepts that don't have a star." She offered gently.

That evening, I went home and reviewed all of the lessons we had covered and found that I was really only struggling in a few. Over the next few days maybe even a week or two, I went to her class after school if I didn't have track practice or during lunch. I was able to fill in the gaps of the concepts that I hadn't fully grasped and get caught up. Additionally, once I got caught up, I leaned a little more to asking for support during the class instead of waiting for Ms. Orchid to invite me to my own private tutoring session during lunch or after school. I did well in her Algebra II class and even took her pre-calculus class the following year. I'm sure you wouldn't be surprised to know that I still periodically keep in touch with her to this day.

Creating a high-quality learning environment means that you as an educator operate as the leader of learning in a classroom setting. You have the opportunity to see in real time if all students are following the cognitive direction of academic learning that you are imparting and if they are not then create a space for them to get caught up. And to be clear, this isn't the transactional, compulsory learning that I am referring to but rather the "light-bulb" moments you see in your students when they deeply understand the teaching. Admittedly, this is probably the principle that I am least experienced to speak on as I can't offer you tons and tons of resources of how to do this well, but I will say adapting a continous improvement mindset will support you along your learning journey. As a practitioner who has had the opportunity to observe many educators in action, I have learned that some of the best educators are always seeking to perfect their craft in one way or the other and practice number five below is perhaps the one that I would encourage you to prioritize after practice number two of creating a student-centered learning environment.

Five Practices to Design High-Quality Educational Learning Environments

Designing high-quality educational learning environments involves intentional planning and consideration of various factors that impact student learning. By considering learner-centered design, fostering inclusivity, incorporating technology appropriately, promoting active engagement, creating a positive classroom climate, and providing access to relevant resources, educators can design high-quality educational learning environments that optimize student learning and promote academic success. Inside every classroom, educators have the opportunity to develop the next generation of critical thinkers who are important members of our society and will one day be at the helm of solving some of our society's largest challenges through their respective fields. Your collective work each year will be a key component of how the students in classrooms today get tracked into the workforce conveyor belt of society. When taking time to carefully observe worforce dynamics, one may notice that Black, Latino/a/x/e and indigenous students have a higher change of being tracked into lower-paying jobs, if not into oppressive systems like incarceration and welfare. But be encouraged because all of these principles, especially Principle 4, support students to reach their fullest potential. Do you strategize on how to deliver your content so that students are at the edge of their seat and will want to beg you to NOT go to recess? Check out some of these strategies to strengthen your practice:

1. **Embed student-centered design**: Truly, no matter the discipline, if you do not design a space, a service, a product for the end user (in a classroom setting this is the student), then, more than likely, you will miss the mark on designing an experience that the user or student will

really enjoy. Trust me, I often have all of these ideas in my head, but when I test my assumptions, I am often surprised by what I learn from my end user. The best approach is to focus on the needs, interests, and abilities of the learners when designing the learning environment. Consider the diverse learning styles, preferences, and abilities of your students, and create an environment that accommodates and supports them. Provide flexible seating options, access to resources, and opportunities for personalization and customization. If your students are too young to give the feedback, engage your fellow teachers to compare and contrast notes on what students enjoy.

2. **Develop a culturally relevant and inclusive learning environment**: Students love to wear shoes that don't fit, said no student ever. Remember how uncomfortable it feels to wear a shoe that doesn't fit and strive to create a learning environment that fits for all of your students. Ultimately your goal is to create an inclusive learning environment that makes students feel welcome and part of the classroom community and where they receive the differentiated instruction they need to access the same quality learning as their peers. One key strategy to do this is by asking them directly. Once you hear from your students, celebrate and value their differences and provide resources and materials that are culturally responsive and relevant. Create opportunities for students to collaborate, share perspectives, and learn from each other's diverse experiences. Students also make excellent teachers.

3. **Embrace a variety of pedagogical approaches**: I cannot tell you how many times I have been to a professional development conference that is a *sit-and-get*. Quick story, I went to a PD that was giving reasons why, as practitioners, we shouldn't just talk *at* people—and guess what? When the PD was finished, that is exactly what happened! We are simply no longer in the era, nor should we have ever been, where we just talk at students. We

must really explore all of the pedagogical approaches that exist, practice and play with them for different lessons, but ultimately, it should be seldom when you as an educator should be standing in front of students just giving information to them.

4. **Incorporate technology appropriately**: The world is changing quickly, and as educators, we must try to change with it. Professions like "influencer" and social media platforms like TikTok or tools like ChatGPT have changed the way students engage with the world, and while there is a clear curriculum that you want to share with them by the end of the year, utilizing the most popular technology will not only make you seem like the cool teacher, it will also serve as tools to enhance learning, engagement, and productivity. As you explore the technology available, select and integrate appropriate technology tools, resources, and platforms that align with the learning goals and objectives. If researchers can use TikTok to gather qualitative data, you can definitely use it to create an engaging learning environment.

5. **Continuously improve your craft**: Like any profession, it takes time and investment to improve your craft. Engage in professional development, observations, and research, obtaining feedback, pursuing higher education, and even peeking at other countries to see how they go about the field of education. Take time to create space for your own self-refelction, seek honest feedback, and become a learner of your craft.

Novela Feature Case Study: New Teacher Seeks Support Designing High-Quality Learning Environments.

Background: Mrs. Gardenia is one of three new teachers that was hired to work at a public elementary school located in a high-poverty community. The majority of the teachers there had more than five years' experience. Additionally, her students come from low-income families facing economic, social, and cultural challenges. Many of her students lack access to resources, opportunities, and support systems outside of school, which can impact their academic performance and well-being. Mrs. Gardenia is committed to using her talents to prepare the next generation of leaders, and her hope is to create a positive and supportive learning environment that meets the diverse needs of her students and helps them thrive despite the challenges they face.

Challenge: Mrs. Gardenia is a new educator who is passionate about creating high-quality educational learning environments for her students in a high-poverty community, but when she did her preservice training, it was at a school with a totally different population. Mrs. Gardenia has tried to utilize all of the training she received in school as well as during her preservice training; however, she still finds herself feeling like the learning environment is not meeting the caliber she dreamed of when she first thought about going into teaching. Oftentimes her students seem disengaged, sleepy, and like they aren't understanding the material.

Application of Principle 4:

One day during Mrs. Gardenia's lesson-planning time, she decided not to go to the shared teacher planning area and instead go to her classroom. The morning had been really tough, and she was disappointed that she had not delivered the lesson the way she had planned it. One of her colleagues Ms. Bee noticed her absence again and went to check on her.

"There you are! We are missing your presence in the teacher conference room. What's going on?" Ms. Bee asked.

"Not much. I just had a tough morning and needed to come to the room to think about what to do better next time," Mrs. Gardenia replied.

"Aww, I definitely understand that. My first few years of teaching, I would retreat to my classroom whenever possible instead of gathering with my colleagues," Ms. Bee said encouragingly.

"Really?" Mrs. Gardenia asked doubtfully.

"Yes, really! And then one day another educator noticed my frequent absence at the teacher gatherings and she came to check on me," said Ms. Bee while she caught a smile on Mrs. Gardenia's face.

"Yeah, it just very different from what I learned in class and even in my preservice," said Mrs. Gardenia defeatedly.

"The first year is always the hardest, but it does get easier with time. And I have to believe this is true with any career as a professional begins to improve their craft," Ms. Bee said encouragingly and then asked, "Have you been leaning into the RYG[6]?"

"The rig?" Ms. Gardenia asked, a bit confused.

"The red, yellow, green flags with your fellow educators," she reminded her.

"Probably, no, maybe? Honestly I am trying a lot of different things and feel overwhelmed," Mrs. Gardenia confessed.

"Well, I definitely want to encourage you to lean into that method for learning and sharing with your colleagues. As an educator, it was always so helpful for me to go see my colleagues in action on their green days. I learned so much from them, and I believe they learned so much from me as well!"

"Aw, yes, I have been so busy that I haven't actually had time in other educators' classrooms, but I appreciate the reminder."

"Of course, just remember the green flag means enter, watch my practice, yellow flag means to come in knowing that your colleague may not be feeling their best or this is an area of growth for them. And, of course, you remember that red is respect the space and come back another day."

Impact on Students:

Engaging and Inclusive Learning Spaces:
Mrs. Gardenia noticed that educators who designed high-quality learning environments had welcoming, inclusive, and engaging learning spaces. She noticed that the design in each classroom had areas for different learning activities, such as reading nooks, collaborative workstations, and hands-on learning stations. The classrooms were decorated with posters, displays, and resources that represented the students' diverse cultures, backgrounds, and experiences, creating a sense of belonging and pride. Mrs. Gardenia also noticed that the classrooms felt safe, organized, and conducive to learning, which helped students feel comfortable and empowered to take ownership of their education.

Implementing Student-Centered Instructional Practices:
Mrs. Gardenia also noticed that classrooms that had high-quality learning environments centered instructional practices on students, and she could see how students had agency over their learning. While not every single lesson she observed was hands-on, interactive, and relevant to her students' lives and interests, she noticed that often they were and there was a strong culture of student-centered practices in her colleagues' approach. She also noticed that her colleagues employed a variety of instructional strategies, such as cooperative learning, inquiry-based learning, and project-based learning, which actively involved their students in the learning process. In her observation, there were plenty of opportunities for student choice, voice,

and agency, allowing them to make decisions about their learning, set goals, and reflect on their progress.

Positive Relationships With Students:
Mrs. Gardenia also noticed that educators in classrooms that designed a high-quality learning environment built positive relationships with their students. She noticed the impact it made in developing a deeper connection with them. Her colleagues took the time to get to know their students as individuals, understanding their interests, strengths, challenges, and aspirations. It was inspiring to see how her peers consistently showed genuine care, empathy, and respect toward their students, treating them with kindness and understanding. Additionally, she noticed how, even when students were being disruptive, they actively listened to their students' concerns, opinions, and ideas and valued their perspectives. Ultimately, the positive relationships her colleagues developed with their students created a sense of trust, belonging, and mutual respect, which strengthened their connection with them and the classroom community.

Summary

Mrs. Gardenia, a new teacher in a high-poverty community, seeks support in designing high-quality learning environments for her students. Despite her training, she feels that her current classroom environment is not meeting her expectations. A colleague encourages her to engage in the red, yellow, green (RYG) method of learning and sharing with fellow educators. Through observation, Mrs. Gardenia learns key practices from her colleagues that positively impact students.

These practices include creating engaging and inclusive learning spaces, where students feel a sense of belonging and take ownership of their education. Student-centered instructional practices, such as hands-on and relevant lessons, provide opportunities for student choice, voice, and agency. Building positive relationships with students and showing genuine care and respect strengthen the connection between teachers and students, fostering trust and a sense of belonging in the classroom community. By implementing these practices, Mrs. Gardenia aims to design a high-quality learning environment for her students despite the challenges they face.

Reflection Questions for Chapter 4—Principle 4: Design High-Quality Educational Learning Environments

1. How do you ensure that your teaching is student-centered, engaging, and aligned with the needs and interests of your learners?
2. What strategies can you implement to build positive relationships and create a culturally responsive learning environment that honors and respects the diversity of your students?
3. What pedagogical approaches do you currently employ in your teaching practice? Are there any other approaches that you have considered exploring or implementing?
4. How can you prioritize and invest in your own professional development to continually enhance your teaching practices?

Notes

1   A refreshing beverage usually made out of fruit, water, and sugar.
2   https://americanart.si.edu/artwork/mans-mind-stretched-new-idea-never-goes-back-its-original-dimension-oliver-wendell-holmes#:~:text=Director's%20Circle-,Man's%20mind%2C%20stretched%20to%20a%20new%20idea%2C%20never%20goes%20back,%E2%80%93%20Oliver%20Wendell%20Holmes

3   https://dschool.stanford.edu/programs/designing-for-social-systems; https://dschool.stanford.edu/news-events/unlocking-the-power-of-design-for-the-social-sector-a-human-centered-systems-minded-and-strategy-aligned-design-approach-for-social-sector-leaders

4   A good resource for teachers: https://fundsofknowledge.org/the-funds-of-knowledge-approach/; https://www.amazon.com/Funds-Knowledge-Theorizing-Households-Communities/dp/0805849181

5   https://shop.scholastic.com/teachers-ecommerce/teacher/search-results.html?text=the%20magic%20school%20bus; https://magicschoolbus.fandom.com/wiki/Valerie_Frizzle

6   The use of red, yellow, green flags to communicate a message with colleagues and/or students to communicate with teachers is a practice I saw in several schools.

5

Principle 5: Partner With Key Stakeholders

My cousin Camila called me excitedly to tell me that she had invented something amazing during her time in college. As I started to congratulate her, she advised me that there was a little problem with her invention. Apparently, the idea was so great others wanted to take it from her. After speaking with her advisors and an intellectual property (IP) attorney, Camila decided that her best way forward was to undergo the IP process for her invention. The only problem was that the entire process was going to cost $10,000.

"Dang, *prima*,[1] congratulations on your invention! I am so proud of you!" I told her.

"Yeah, but I don't know where I am going to get the money from," she replied sadly.

"Can you get a loan?" I tried to help her generate options. Apparently, my brilliant cousin had already thought through all of the alternatives, but none of them seemed viable at that current moment. Especially not asking our parents for a loan as it was both unrealistic that they would have the money as well as be willing to loan it for something extremely unknown like an IP process.

"Prima, help me think about creative ways we can make money. After all, isn't that what you got your degree in?" she jabbed at me.

DOI: 10.4324/9781003401018-6

"Yeah, but I just can't make $10,000 out of thin air. There is a whole journey you need to go through to create a viable product for the market," I said as I started to explain the process of entrepreneurship and she cut me off exasperated and with a huge flood of excitement.

"Prima, I know what we can do!" she said excitedly.

"Oh god, here we go," I said.

Camila is my "ride or die" cousin, and there hasn't been anything we haven't done for one another. We grew up in the same neighborhood and attended the same elementary school, and despite this, Camila, like myself, tremendously beat the odds.

"Tamales. We can make tamales," she said, chuckling not even believing what was coming out of her mouth.

The thing about Camila and me is that our families supported us tremendously to not fall into the typical roles that Latina girls in our family were subjected to. We were never forced to do much of the chores at the house nor cook, thankfully, and to our siblings disapproval. But that literally meant that neither she nor I had much experience flipping a tortilla with our bare hands (because that is a thing in our family) much less making tamales and certainly not $10,000 worth of tamales.

"Camila," I said laughing. "You are joking right? There is no way you or I are capable of making tamales," I said trying to be serious with her because this idea was quickly becoming a possibility.

"We got this girl. Let's talk to our mamas and our *tias*[2] and tell them why we need their help, and I am sure they will help us out," she said excitedly.

"Okay, as long as we don't have to make the actual tamales, you can count me in," I told her. "After all, I can use my business administration skills to administer the money we get," I laughed.

A few days later, Camila told me the great news that our family was willing to help, but there was a small catch. And, of course, that catch meant that they expected the both of us to learn how to make tamales and help them out. Since I had already graduated and she was near to graduation, they didn't see a reason for us not to help in the kitchen anymore.

The details of when I agreed to make 12,500 tamales in one weekend are still blurry. But what is more clear than the various batches of *masa*[3] we made is that our family and our community came together to help us make over 12,500 tamales and fundraise $10,000 in one weekend so Camila could afford her IP application! There were certainly different ways that we could have made money, but it was absolutely beautiful to see that my cousin had a need to fundraise $10,000 to protect her idea and our family and community had nothing but support. Our family, friends, and community partnered in such a strong way to achieve the goal, and even though no one really had $10,000 dollars, everyone had something they could offer.

Principle 5: Partner With Key Stakeholders

Strong partnerships between families, educators, and community members can be the difference between a student beating the odds or cycling into generational poverty. And while my story is a great story that resulted in a great ending, it is not the dominant story. There is a catalytic opportunity for educators to deeply connect with the families, community members, and other key stakeholders that support students. Not only is it the right thing to do, but 50 years of growing research prove the benefit of partnership between educators and families. Currently the dominant narrative around partnering with families and community members to support students outcomes is that "it's another thing educators have to do." When in reality, the dominant narrative should be that educators, families, and community members are on the same team and partnership is critical for the success of students.

Do you remember in Chapter 1 when I showed you Urie Bronfenbrenner's ecological systems theory model? Take a moment to go back to Figure 0.1 to look inside the microsystem again. Yes, you, my dear educator, do, in fact, hold a very special place in the lives of students. And yes, according to the ecological systems theory, there are a handful of other special people that are also part of the innermost circle of those who have the opportunity to make an impact in the life of a student. The reason we say "parent and family" is because we all know that not every student has the same familial makeup, and that is okay. Every student has people in their innermost circle to support and champion their dreams. And just like a chair, the more legs it has, the stronger and more capacity it has to lift up a student. Individually each stakeholder in the life of a student has a unique position and a distinct opportunity to make an impact in the life of a student, and collectively, their impact is multiplied.

Remember in chapter 2 how I told you my mom resolved the issue of not understanding English well enough for my math homework. Just like my cousin Camilia, my mom leveraged her commumity. Sometimes we think that we need expensive and complex solutions to support students who come from marginilized communities, but we should trust that families have what they need in their community and this short memory further elevates this idea.

***

It was a beautiful sunny day in Austin, Texas, and the school bus had just dropped me off at the large pecan tree in front of our building. As I walked through our apartment door, my mother was standing in our small kitchen cooking refried beans, again. I walked past her briskly and threw my backpack on the brown carpet in our living room where my little sister was playing with her dolls and started stomping over to our shared bedroom.

Before I got to my room that had nothing but a bed and sheets and a beat-up brown dresser with secondhand clothes hanging in the closet, my mom yelled, "Marcela *qué te pasa?*" *What is wrong?*

I turned around and looked at her with piercing eyes and gritting my teeth, I said, "Nothing, you can't help me. You don't speak English."

If I could have unpacked for her what I was really trying to say, it would be something like, "This sucks, I hate being poor, I hate not having a father, I hate that we can't eat the food we want only the food that is shamefully labeled WIC,[4] I hate that I don't understand Spanish (my native tongue) and that English is hard for me, I hate everything about my life."

With a stoic look and tears streaming down her face, she asked me again.

This time with an even more acidic tone and tears streaming from my face, I yelled, "I am stupid! I can't do my homework, and you can't help me because you don't speak English and you never have time since Papa left. You are always working."

I was still sugarcoating my feelings. But my mother understood my problem. She knew if she didn't do something, I would fail.

She looked me square in the eyes, and with her eyes welling with tears eyes, she said, "*Marcela, me romperé mi espalda para asegurarme que recibas una educación.*" Even though "Marcela, I will break my back to make sure you get an education" is translated word for word, it doesn't do just do justice to the Spanish version.

She turned off the stove and went next door to our neighbor's house. "Valeria, Valeria, open the door," she exclaimed. "I need your help!"

My mother's exasperation was palpable. Valeria came out of her small apartment, "Lina, what is wrong?"

"I need you to help Marcela. She needs you now." Valeria's expression quickly turned to one of deep concern.

"Is she okay?" she asked.

"Yes, yes she's fine, but she can't do her homework," my mother answered.

"Ay Lina, you scared me. I thought something serious had happened to her."

"No, no she just needs help with her homework. The math problems are now word problems, and she says she doesn't understand the English. I don't know how to help her," said my mother explaining the situation.

For the next couple of years, Valeria helped me with my homework and my English, and my love of math continued.

In sharing this story, I'd love to lift up to frameworks/theories that educators can use in their practice. First is community asset mapping. We have to trust that communities have the answers to the most pressing problems they are facing and sometimes it may just require our encouragement to lean into the resources within one's own community. Out of desperation, my mom knocked on Valeria's door for her to support me with my homework. In communities, how many more Valeria's are there? What role can we play to encourage families to tap into the community assets that may have access to literally next door? Secondly, funds of knowledge. Every family has knowledge and life lessons to share with their student from the custodian to the CEO and as educators, one of our roles is to figure out how to weave in the rich and diverse knowledge families and communities have with dignity and respect into our curriculum.

To truly create educational equity, we have the opportunity to encourage families to become strong educational partners and create a collaborative space that invites them to use the tools we have to navigate the educational system and in turn allows them to share the tools they have to support their students. We are experts in education and we know the system. We must connect with families and communities in a way that says to them, "I see you!" and I need and want what you bring to the table to support your student.

To advance the mission of creating educational equality across the nation, educators have the opportunity to partner with and encourage families (and communities) to take their seat at the education table and together navigate the educational system to provide strategic guidance, coaching, resources, and support to champion the dreams of students.

Educators foot in the door to do this very important work is through deeply connecting with a student beyond academics and doing a few key things. First, really taking time to understand who a student's ecosystem of support is comprised of. To do this, I personally like using the ecological systems theory model because it is a clear visual of groups of folks who support students. Next, work to understand what relationships already exist between the supporters. This one is a little more complex, because it will require that you first take time to build a relationship with a student to get access to this information. Once a relationship is established with a student, I think you could use a variation of Jody Hoffer Gittell's Relational Coordination work to help map out the relationships and even the health of relationships that exist in a student's life. Finally, work to build a relationship with the variety of stakeholders who are already supporting a student's learning and development. It's kinda like a baseball game, educators are coming in during different innings and it's imperative that you understand there are more players on the field to help the student win and ultimately the feeling among all the players on the field is that everyone should be playing on the same team.

Each student has their own complex ecosystem that has made them who they are and will ultimately give shape to their life. You are in a student's microsystem,[5] one of the closest connections of influence and trust.

Your special position of power and privilege to orient children, their families, and their communities to reach new horizons of dreams and ultimately their potential gives you an incredible platform to have life-changing and generational impact. So, remember how I said that the dominant narrative is that engaging with families is just another thing educators have to do? If we treat it in that way, it will certainly become another thing we have to do.

***

It was the spring, and all school staff were gearing up for the testing season. My task list seemed endless, and I felt a bit overwhelmed with everything that needed to be done over the course of the next few days, but I was excited that it was Friday afternoon and that a weekend of rest was upon us. As I was knocking things off my list, I got a call from the front office that a mom was very upset and requested to speak with someone right away. The mom was Spanish-speaking, and I was the only person available to meet with her. The mother had come to pull her son from the school because he had consistently failed his standardized testing practice tests. We took withdrawals very seriously, and obviously, my goal was to ensure he stayed enrolled. From the moment I walked in the room, I knew the meeting was going to be intense because of the determined look on her face, the same one I remember seeing on my mother decades before.

We conversed in Spanish. She said, "Ms. Andrés, let's not waste time. I am withdrawing my son from the school."

"Why?" I asked

Her response rocked my career choice to be in education.

"I don't feel supported or respected as a partner in my student's education. I don't know how to support my son in school, and the school is not helping me. In my country, Mexico, I know how to move like a fish in water. I know how the school system works and what support I need to give my student. But here, my hands are tied. I don't understand this system, and the little I do understand is confusing and feels like I am a nuisance instead of a partner in my student's education. How are you going to help me not feel like that?"

She went on to explain she had just found weeks of failed practice exams in her student's backpack and was upset that not even one teacher or anyone from administration (and that included me) had called to suggest that she bring him in for tutoring and that testing was next week. She also shared that she had called the school and had requested to speak with any of Juan's teachers, but had never received a call back.

"Testing is next week, and Juan is not ready to take the state tests and no one has helped him. How are you going to help me advocate for my student?

She paused with tears filling her eyes after asking the question. I let her speak, and the exchange with her made me reminisce about my parent-teacher conferences as a student. I could picture my mother sitting in front of my non-Spanish–speaking teachers, not sure what to say or do—exactly what this mother was describing to me. The difference was, with me, this mom was able to express herself freely in her native language and was able to tell me exactly how she felt and what had happened. My pause was perhaps too long. The memory of my moms eyes welling out of desperation were evoked by our interaction.

"I am withdrawing him and taking him to a school that takes the time to communicate with me to truly partner with me in ensuring he receives a high-quality education. He will probably fail the state test this year, but I will make sure that never happens again."

I wanted to defend our school, our administrators, myself our educators, but she was right—we had not partnered with her, we had not honored her place as a key partner in the education of her student, and more than likely, Juan would, in fact, fail the state tests next week. With just the weekend left before the exams, there wasn't much anyone could do. Somewhere in the line of communication between the educators, administrators, and other support staff, Juan's failing grades had gotten lost. We had relied on the multiple notes we sent home with Juan to make it to his mother's hands. We infact were not playing baseball as a true team ensuring that each plate was covered.

Over the course of the next few days, especially as I administered the tests and saw Juan's empty seat, I thought deeply about her question: *How are you going to help me advocate for my student?*

Although I didn't have an answer for her that day, I knew that I needed to find one for her and every parent and family that entrusts us with their children's future, especially the families who are unfamiliar with the U.S. education system it was the last solid utterance of my why. I later learned that there was a break in communication between one of his teachers and the front office. The teacher that the mom had been calling had received the calls, but when she went to the front office to ask for help to call home with a translator, either no one was available or no one was able to speak Spanish. With everything the teacher had on her plate with testing, she had just simply forgotten to keep following up and effective systems of communication were not in place to follow-up with her consistently.

The environment was not conducive for deep partnership among the educators and the families, and while the school had good systems in place, they hadn't been good enough to support and foster partnership between Juan mama and his educators. As educators, I know we want great things for students like me and like Juan, who have the odds set against them. As educators, I know we want them to reach their wildest dreams because we all know it is possible.

The question is, have created school cultures in our classrooms that elevate the critical nature of partnership between the people who love and support students the most?

Five Practices to Partner with Key Stakeholders

Partnering with key stakeholders, including parents, caregivers, administrators, and the broader community, is crucial for creating a supportive and effective educational environment. Effective partnerships require ongoing effort and collaboration to ensure the best outcomes for students. In our society, we need to find a systemic solution to that mother's question—*how are you going to help me advocate for my student?*—for *every* student. Students are an extension of their families and community. Imagine graduation day for every student; imagine everyone who will show up for them to celebrate their success as they walk the stage to receive their diploma. If it is difficult for you to imagine who will show up for your students, take a moment to think about everyone who showed up for you and/or supported you. Children have a beautiful network of support, even if it varies by its composition. Parents, foster-care parents, grandparents, guardians, aunts, uncles, cousins, church leaders, mentors, and educators are inside of a student's most intimate circle of support. Educators are the experts as it pertains to curriculum,[6] and the other key stakeholders in this circle are the experts as it pertains to the whole student.

Often the narrative we play into in education is that families should engage with educators, when in actuality it is educators who should engage with families and the other key stakeholders in the lives of children. Children invest six to eight hours of their days in "learning" inside of a classroom, but as any great educator knows, learning is always happening all around us. The power of engaging with a student's family and community is unparalleled to what stand-alone teaching, even when it is culturally responsive, can ever accomplish. Remember the special position of an educator? The other key stakeholders are families, and community members are also key partners in the lives of students. It is imperative that educators understand that a handful of other stakeholders also share a special proximate position in the lives of students. There are many tools and resources that can guide educators to strengthen their partnerships with stakeholders. A leader that has deeply impacted my practice and leadership is Dr. Karen Mapp, a senior lecturer on education at the Harvard Graduate School of Education and the faculty Director of the Education Policy and Management Master's Program. Truly one of the only reasons I applied to Harvard was to study under her leadership. Dr. Mapp has authored several books on family and community engagement and she is the brilliant mind behind the Dual Capacity Framework that delineates the roadmap of partnership from challenges to outcomes in to the most linear way and yet manages to drive home the fact that building relationships is anything but linear and complex. Her leadership and instruction are deeply embedded into my practice. As I work with leaders across the nation, I utilize the Dual Capacity framework as one of my cornerstone tools. When I work with educators, I use the following five practices to provide a high-level how-to road map to actualize partnership from idea to implementation.

1. **Identify the stakeholders in a student's ecosystem**: One of the key reasons we say family instead of parent is that students have a variety of different important people who love and support them, not just their biological parents. When we think about all of the special people in the lives of students, with educators certainly being one of them, we must also take time to understand who is supporting the student when they are not in our classrooms. As educators, the more we understand a student's ecosystem of support, the better we can partner with them. Two easy ways to do this are to take inventory of who is in a students ecosystem one is to map out/request the student to map out their circle of support. There are several activities you can creatively use to get a better understanding of the people closest to students. A second way to further understand who supports the student outside of the classroom is to use a framework called relational coordination (Gittell). This framework can give you an insight into the ways that individuals closest to a student support their academic learning and development. The first framework is to map out who is in their system of support and the second framework is to really understand how the relationships in the life of a student playout. This framework is used in a variety of ways, but definitely one way I like to use it is when I work with leaders to identify the network of support that surround students in a school. Through a class project, you could easily create a similar activity where you gather insights on the network of people who support your students and deteremine the importance and health of the relationship.

2. **Engage in a variety of outreach strategies**: Before you get to the next very important practice of building trust,

you must first make the courageous effort to reach out to stakeholders in a student ecosystem. Phone calls, emails, letters, notes, TikToks, whatever you feel most comfortable with, develop strategies to reach out to the stakeholders in your student's life to make an introduction of who you are and ask to partner with them. This may be your very first year teaching their student, and it is you, as an educator, that is partnering with them on their student's journey. Now this is perhaps one of the scariest steps. Cite this idea to The Essential Conversation, Sara Lawrence-Lightfoot. There are only two wrong ways to reach out to families. First, not reach out at all and second, with an attitude or dispostion that you do this work alone. If you humbly reach out acknowledging that you celebrate and want to partner with the other special people in the life of your student, it will be well-received.

3. **Build relationships based on trust and respect**: Once you have reached out to stakeholders in your student's ecosystem work on building relationships based on trust, respect, and mutual understanding. Listen to their perspectives, concerns, and feedback with an open mind and respond with empathy and respect. One of my favorite part of listenting to Dr. Mapp explain the Dual Capacity Framework is how she pauses with deep intentionallity when she explains that building trust is foundational. It seems like such a simple concept, but as anyone who has a relationship with another person knows, building and keeping trust is something you have to actively work at and in a school setting with its vast complexities, it is that much more difficult, but not impossible.

4. **Establish open and transparent communication channels**: In almost every school I visit, communication is still a growth area between families and educators regardless of the technology available. While technology is a great tool, remember that it is just that, a tool. Communication happens when people engage in dialogue. When working with families, seek to establish open and transparent communication channels with key stakeholders to foster regular and effective communication. When communicating with families, consider making it a priority to

provide updates on student progress, share information about classroom activities and assignments, and welcome the opportunity to listen to concerns or feedback.

5. **Co-create engagement strategies with stakeholders**: Similar to asking students their input to design a high-quality learning environment, you should also consider working with stakeholders to co-create the strategies they will find most meaningful and relevant to the partnership. Too often I see a copy and paste of strategies from the prior year improvement plan or calendar of events, and we are surprised when families do not come to the school. The more you ask individuals for their input, the more likely they are to engage with you.

Novela Feature Case Study: Enhancing Family and Community Engagement in Middle School

Background: Mrs. Petunia is a dedicated and enthusiastic teacher who recently transitioned from teaching fourth grade to sixth grade at a public middle school. In her previous teaching experience, she had a strong partnership with families who actively volunteered in the classroom and school events. However, since moving up to middle school, Mrs. Petunia has noticed a significant decline in family involvement. This has left her feeling disappointed and concerned about the lack of engagement from her students' families.

Challenge: Mrs. Petunia is disheartened by the decrease in family participation and recognizes the importance of fostering a strong home-school connection. She believes that involving families in the educational journey positively impacts student success and overall school culture. However, she is unsure about how to effectively engage families in middle school, where the level of involvement tends to taper off. Mrs. Petunia is determined to find a solution that

goes beyond traditional volunteering and creates meaningful opportunities for family and community engagement.

Application of Principle 5:

During a conversation with her colleague, Mr. Rodriguez,
Mrs. Petunia expresses her frustration about the lack of family
involvement in her classroom. Mr. Rodriguez explains that
it is common for family engagement to diminish in middle
school but assures her that there are alternative approaches
to engage families effectively. He suggests that Mrs. Petunia
review the year's scope and sequence and identify opportunities to design family and community engagement activities aligned with the curriculum.

Inspired by Mr. Rodriguez's advice, Mrs. Petunia embarks
on designing a series of interactive and meaningful activities
that involve families and the community in her sixth-grade
curriculum. She organizes a family reading night where
parents and students come together to read and discuss a
selected book. She also establishes a community partnership with a local museum, arranging a field trip that connects
with the social studies curriculum. Additionally, Mrs. Petunia
encourages families to participate in classroom presentations,
where students showcase their projects and learning to their
parents and to build even stronger partnership, Mrs. Petunia
finds creative and culturally relevant ways to gather families
insights on their preferred ways of partnership.

Impact on Students:

Linked to Learning:
Through Mrs. Petunia's efforts to enhance family and community engagement, the students experience a positive shift

in their educational environment. The involvement of families in activities such as family reading night strengthens the connection between home and school, reinforcing the importance of literacy and fostering a love for reading. The field trip to the museum expands students' understanding of the social studies topics and helps them make real-world connections. The classroom presentations provide students with the opportunity to share their achievements with their families, boosting their self-confidence and sense of accomplishment.

Student Motivation and Behavior:
Mrs. Petunia also notices an improvement in student motivation and behavior, as the presence of engaged families creates a supportive and encouraging atmosphere. The involvement of families enhances the sense of community within the classroom, promoting a collaborative learning environment where students feel valued and supported.

Increased Cultural Awareness and Appreciation:
By involving families and community members in classroom activities, Mrs. Petunia exposes her students to diverse perspectives, cultures, and experiences. The participation of families from different backgrounds and the community partnership with the local museum broaden students' understanding of the world around them. They gain a deeper appreciation for the richness of cultural diversity and develop empathy toward others. This exposure helps create a more inclusive and accepting classroom environment where students value and respect one another's differences.

Strengthened Academic Support:
Through family and community engagement activities, Mrs. Petunia establishes stronger lines of communication and

collaboration between parents, students, and herself. This open dialogue allows parents to gain a better understanding of the curriculum and classroom expectations. As a result, they are better equipped to provide academic support and reinforce learning at home. Students benefit from the increased involvement of their families, receiving additional guidance and resources outside of the classroom. The strengthened academic support network positively impacts their learning outcomes and overall academic success.

Summary

In this case study, Mrs. Petunia, a new sixth-grade teacher, faces the challenge of declining family involvement in middle school. With the guidance of her colleague Mr. Rodriguez, she explores alternative ways to engage families beyond traditional volunteering. By reviewing the year's scope and sequence, Mrs. Petunia designs family and community engagement activities aligned with the curriculum. Through initiatives like family reading night, community field trips, and classroom presentations, she successfully fosters a stronger home-school connection. As a result, students benefit from increased motivation, improved behavior, and a sense of belonging within the classroom community.

Reflection Questions for Chapter 5—Principle 5: Partner with Key Stakeholders

1. What strategies can you implement to build positive relationships with your students and create a supportive environment that nurtures their aspirations?
2. How can you actively learn about the ecosystem of support in the lives of your students to better understand their needs and aspirations?

3. How can you effectively communicate to the stakeholders in the lives of your students that you are excited to be in partnership with them? What strategies can you implement to establish clear lines of communication and foster open, collaborative relationships with key stakeholders?

4. How can you design and implement activities or events that actively involve key stakeholders in the educational process? How can you facilitate meaningful interactions and collaborations among key stakeholders to collectively support the hopes and dreams of your students?

Notes

1   Cousin.
2   Aunts.
3   Maize dough.
4   WIC means the Special Supplemental Nutrition Program for Women, Infants and Children authorized by section 17 of the Child Nutrition Act of 1966, 42 U.S.C. 1786.
5   Urie Bronfenbrenner's ecological system theory.
6   I learned this concept from my time partnering with the leaders at Garland Independent School District.

6

Oxygen Masks Are Not Just for Airplanes

It is estimated that approximately 25,000 flights carrying a little over 2.3 million passengers take place in the United States per day.[1] If you have ever been on a flight, then you know shortly after the door closes, a flight attendant will begin the preflight safety briefings. Whether you are flying over water or staying inland, the briefing will always include a portion about oxygen masks. The script usually runs something like, "*Should the cabin experience sudden pressure loss, stay calm and listen for instructions from the cabin crew. Oxygen masks will drop down from above your seat. Place the mask over your mouth and nose, like this. Pull the strap to tighten it. If you are traveling with children, make sure that your own mask is on first before helping your children.*" If there were ever a true emergency, this frequently repeated script would dramatically increase the chances of a passenger's survival. Our lives depend on the breaths we take, and thus, the safety aviation crews know that to support others in their flight journey in case of an emergency, a passenger must first support themselves.

In the journey of education, the oxygen safety protocols are the same. There are over 49 million students in PK-12 classrooms today taking a learning journey led by just over 3 million educators.[2] In order for educators to truly support a rich, high-quality learning experience, they must be receiving oxygen first. Educators play a critical role in shaping the lives of their students,

DOI: 10.4324/9781003401018-7

often dedicating themselves to the betterment of their students' education and well-being. However, in the midst of their selfless efforts, educators often neglect their own well-being, putting their own "oxygen masks" last. This neglect can lead to burnout, decreased job satisfaction, and ultimately, diminished effectiveness in the classroom. For educators to truly create a deeper connection with their students, it is important for educators to prioritize self-care as a fundamental aspect of effective teaching and explore practical strategies that can be implemented to ensure educators are taking care of themselves for the benefit of their students.

Children don't get to pick the circumstances they were born into—as a matter of fact, none of us do. Yet, every student's life is a masterpiece, and educators are privileged to take part in supporting them to realize their fullest potential. Every student's circumstance is wildly different, and only through building a meaningful relationship with them will educators deeply know what conditions a student is learning in and what supports they currently have and need to be successful. Sadly, sometimes those supports come with adverse childhood experiences (ACEs) and many educators are not properly trained to handle things that come their way.

I was a student with trauma. Trauma is ugly. It made me feel things that were untrue and tainted my reality in a way that made me feel less than. When my father left, I felt like something was terribly wrong with me. I would wait desperately by the phone to receive a call from him in hopes he would say, "I love you and I am sorry for leaving you and your sister." Every time there was a knock at the door, I would run to open it in hopes that it would be him with his arms wide open saying, "I am back." Yet that never happened. Instead, his abandonment was a domino effect of the series of traumas I would experience but thankfully have worked through as an adult and through reconciliation with him.

Despite my trauma and the trauma kids face today, every student deserves to dream big and have champions in their corner. The educators in my life connected with me as a human being, as a student who had dreams within my being and deserved to live out my purpose. They were some of the strongest champions

I had in my corner to help me see a world beyond my reality. When my mom remarried and we moved to Pflugerville, I had found the transition extremely difficult.

In the old "school" model, learners were more positioned as obedient, passive recipients. Adults would set the direction, while students would comply or face punishment. However, in new models, young people have opportunities to be active drivers of their learning and leaders within their community. Learners drive their unique paths—moving at their own pace (based on mastery) and modalities through learning goals that matter to them while shaping the broader learning community.

By surrounding themselves with encouraging, important, loving people, kids can develop life skills and habits that follow them into their adult lives.

But the adults in the lives of children have to have their oxygen mask on first. Here is the thing about education—emergency events like gas leaks, fires, or devastating events such as mass school shootings—don't happen every day, thankfully, so as an educator you may not feel the pressure or need to put on your oxygen mask to support students unless there is a more pronounced emergency.

The problem is that our education system has been in an emergency status for a long time. From weathering the effects of poverty, secondhand trauma, inadequate funding, and need for medical support on top of the academic disparities of students, especially those that come from some of our most vulnerable communities, schools triage emergencies all day, every day, and our teachers are the frontline responders. Because of the frequency and commonality of these emergencies, they have become non-threatening emergencies that most educators may not respond to with the same level of urgency to put on their oxygen masks. Now stack the nonthreatening emergencies on top of the residual trauma to an educator's psyche from life-threatening events like school shootings and COVID. An educator not wearing a mask is either probably leaving the field of education or suffocating. We are living in times where our education systems are in an emergency, and educators must have their oxygen masks first to support themselves before they support students.

Our nation has become increasingly divisive and politicized. Unfortunately the division and policies being thrown around are just more decoys deflecting attention from the real issue at hand—not all children, especially those from our most vulnerable communities, which are predominantly Black and Latino, are able to realize their fullest potential with access to a high-quality education. This issue isn't new. We have historically oppressed and intentionally cycled students with these demographics into generational poverty. And we as a society will continue to do so unless educators everywhere make a bold commitment to advance educational equity. I humbly offer the five principles as a framework that can change outcomes for students across the country if we create deeper connections with them.

Educators are the experts as it pertains to their curriculum and context. You know exactly what every student needs to realize their fullest potential, and my hope is that you will adopt these principles to realize a deeper connection with your students.

During one of my travels abroad, I had the privilege of visiting an orphanage in Kumasi, Ghana. In addition to noticing the wonderful care they provided to the children, I was struck by the concept of a village parent. Every group of children had a village parent who cared and loved them. This idea of village support was so profound to me and made me think about how educators are an integral part of a student's village.

While educators are not a student's parent or guardian, they have a very special role in the lives of children. Educators impart knowledge while also serving as a key partner to a family in the social-emotional development of a student. Shortly after we went into shutdown during the pandemic and after I checked on all of my family members, I began to reach out to educators who I have kept in contact with over the years. After inquiring about how they and their families were doing, I would ask about their students and their families. And almost resoundingly, every educator I spoke with had accounted for the majority of their students' well-being. Two things that struck me during my conversations with educators during the COVID crisis were that the majority of my conversations were not frantic and that educators, beyond accounting for their students, knew what each student's life situation was. Because of the need to convert to digital over-night, they knew whether a student had access to technology or if they would need to make short-term modifications until technology became available. But in addition to the technology, educators also knew whether their students were eating three meals a day and inquiring about their life situation. They knew if students' parents were essential workers serving our country and also how they were being cared for during the day. The level of connection grew organically during the pandemic.

I think that the reason the level of connection was deeper with students and families during the pandemic is because educators were first able to take care of themselves and their own fam-ilies. Once their oxygen masks were on, they were able to extend their care and attention to their students and families. Although COVID and its many variants have become a thing of everyday life, with the physical return to schools, many educators have left their oxygen masks at home. They have run into the halls of schools ready to do what they do best, educate children, but they have left their oxygen masks at home.

Our education system needs courageous, confident, and highly qualified educators to lead the charge of educating our children. In order for you to be all those things, you must take care of yourself first.

Five Practices to Put Your Oxygen Mask On

If I were to write a country song, I would call it "Educators and Entrepreneurs!" Whew, since I have been in both of these roles, I can wholeheartedly tell you that self-care is the last thing on our to-do list. But may the flight attendant's message, however over-repeated it is, remind us that as educators, it is important to prioritize self-care to ensure that we are able to fully support our students. Remember, taking care of yourself is not selfish but rather a necessary step to ensure that you are in the best mental, emotional, and physical state to fully support your students. By prioritizing self-care, educators can better manage stress, maintain their well-being, and be more effective in their roles as teachers, be more joyful, have more balance, and ultimately benefit their students as well. Here are some self-care activities that educators can practice to take care of their own well-being:

1. **Practice mindfulness**: Engage in mindfulness practices. Pause, breathe, reflect. Take time to engage in deep breathing exercise, meditation, or yoga to help reduce stress, increase self-awareness, and promote mental well-being. Mindfulness can help you stay present and focused, manage stress, and enhance your overall well-being.

2. **Set boundaries**: Set clear boundaries between work and personal time to avoid burnout. Avoid taking work home or working excessively long hours. Make sure to prioritize self-care and personal time to engage in activities that bring you joy and help you recharge. And sometimes the number one person you have to set boundaries with is yourself—saying no to others so you can say yes to your self-care is okay!

3. **Exercise and stay active**: This one is a hard one for me, but each time I finish a workout, I truly feel great. Engage in regular physical activity to help reduce stress, improve your mood, and increase your energy levels. Find physical activities that you enjoy, such as walking, jogging, swimming, or practicing a sport and make time for regular exercise in your routine. I personally enjoy listening to my audiobooks while I am taking my dogs for a walk.

4. **Connect with others**: The joy that comes with being around people who brighten your day is priceless. Take time to build and maintain meaningful connections with friends, family, and colleagues. Spend time with loved ones, engage in social activities, and seek support from trusted individuals when needed. Connecting with others can help reduce stress, promote a sense of belonging, and provide emotional support. And if COVID taught us anything, it is that life is fragile and we need deep connection.

5. **Get adequate sleep**: This is also one that I struggle with but again can't emphasize enough that when you are

rested you feel better. Prioritize getting enough restful sleep each night. Lack of sleep can impact your mood, cognitive function, and overall well-being.

Reflection Questions for Chapter 6—Oxygen Masks Are Not Just for Airplanes

1. How can you proactively identify and address any signs of neglecting self-care to ensure you are taking care of yourself consistently?
2. How can you incorporate self-care practices into your daily routine to ensure you are taking care of your physical, mental, and emotional well-being?
3. Have you established an accountability self-care circle with your colleagues and administrators to support each other in prioritizing self-care? How has this circle helped you be accountable for taking care of yourself?
4. Have you identified the support you need from your school administrators to prioritize self-care? Have you communicated these needs to them and sought their assistance in creating a conducive environment for self-care? How can you work collaboratively with your administrators to ensure that self-care is prioritized in your school community?

Notes

1   https://www.whitehouse.gov/wp-content/uploads/2023/03/03 2023-National-Aeronautics-ST-Priorities.pdf; https://bocacenter.com/ark-single/how-many-domestic-flights-per-day-in-the-us
2   https://nces.ed.gov/fastfacts/display.asp?id=372

7

The Power of Human Connection

Life is full of connections. And the educators in our schools have a very special place of power and privilege that can impact the lives of current students and generations to come. Everyone has a role to play in the life of a student, and in a trying time like this in education, no matter how challenging the work gets, we have to remember our humanity.

When I started writing this book, I found myself in Salt Lake City, Utah, at a super chill coffee shop called Nostalgia. It has been a few years since the world abruptly came to a stop almost overnight because of the COVID-19 virus. While I was experiencing absolutely zero nostalgia to re-experience the trauma living through a global pandemic brought, I recognized that perhaps it served as a catalyst to further connect us as human beings. I mean, when else prior to the pandemic did you reach out to neighbors for basic necessities like toilet paper? Too soon?

What we collectively lived through was difficult for all of us—from minor inconveniences to the tragic deaths of our loved ones and our inability to mourn in community. As we continue to work to return to "normal," there is an opportunity to not squander the shared lived experiences, however difficult, that the pandemic offered us and reimagine how we deeply connect with one another. Especially in the hallways of schools.

Educators, better than anyone, know that schools are the public institutions that weave the lives of communities together. Schools create the space for students, families, and educators to

DOI: 10.4324/9781003401018-8

come together as strangers and leave as community members of a larger society. As the late Nelson Mandela once said,[1] education is, in fact, the most powerful weapon to change the world. Educators have the power to transform the lives of their students, families, and ultimately communities through the knowledge they impart and connections they make.

Educators like you changed my life through developing a deeper connection with me in their classrooms, but it was really only later in my life that I saw the power of connection to my life, family legacy, and now my own personal legacy.

Shortly after my first visit to Salt Lake City, I learned that my firm was awarded a contract to develop a strategic plan with an amazing nonprofit organization dedicated to advancing the voices of young people through arts and media.

I sat at my aunt's inviting dinner table and excitedly shared with her the details of our new project and that I would be traveling to Utah.

"U-t-ah," she repeated back with a reminiscing tone and glossy eyes. "U-t-ah," she repeated again.

"*Si*, tia, Utah. Have you been?" I asked.

"No," she replied and took a long deep breath and exhaled. "But your *abuelo* Marcelo, he was a *bracero,* and he picked apples and apricots in U-t-ah." She repeated the name again as she gave a deep, long sigh.

"In Utah?" I asked rhetorically, marveling at the significance of what she was sharing with me. I am his legacy, and by doing work in a state where he tilled the land, I was literally and figuratively reaping his harvest. My grandfather Marcelo was a *bracero,* or immigrant agricultural worker, in Utah. He was the first person in my family to work in the United States. He picked apples and apricots for pennies on the dollar because of the extreme poverty that my family from Mexico experienced. And I, his granddaughter, would also be working in Utah but as the CEO of my own company!

And just like the land my grandfather once cared for and the harvest I get to enjoy today, these blessings and others beyond my wildest dreams are because of educators like you. Educators planted seeds in my life that helped cycle me out of generational poverty; they connected with me to create a deeper relationship.

When opening up four schools in one of Austin's most underserved communities, I found myself exhausted almost every day after a long day of work. Opening a school, much less four at the same time, is not for the faint of heart, and it takes a lot of focus and dedication coupled with repeatable processes to create efficiency and structure. With a high-demanding role, I found myself needing a creative outlet after work. I loved running, but when I ran miles on the trail, I would always start thinking through all the things that I needed to do or improve on when I returned to school. One day, while speaking with my friends, they invited me to go dancing to salsa music. At first, I was a little resistant to go dancing with them because stereotypically I thought I was supposed to know how to dance because I have Latin blood running through my veins, but the truth was that growing up, we didn't do much dancing in my home and my experiences with dancing had been limited. One of my friends noticed my resistance and encouraged me to go anyway. She said that we would have a great time and that we could get there early enough to catch the dance lesson to polish our dancing skills and also scope out good dance partners. Receiving a refresh on dancing sounded like a perfect strategy to me, so I agreed and we went dancing for the first time. During the class, I was so rigid. The instructor would clap out the beats and model for us how to move our hips and body to the rhythm of the music, but I was too focused on the process that I kept missing the beat. Regardless, as a high-achieving person, I was determined to figure out the dance process and keep at it. My friends and I would return several times to the same dance studio, and each time I became more frustrated with my inability to dance to the rhythm of the music and would often just sit on the sidelines and watch them enjoy themselves dancing. Until one day when I was sitting and watching them dance and a man who introduced himself by the name of Guillermo asked me to dance. I kindly declined his offer to dance and told him that I didn't know how to dance very well. He chuckled and said, "I know. I've seen you a few times here and it looks like you are not having fun." I laughed—he was right. This creative outlet was starting to feel like the second shift in my already long day. I was so in my head about the steps that I was not enjoying the moment or the music. As we were dancing, I kept replaying the sound beats in my head, watching other people dance, and trying my hardest to stay on beat. Then Guillermo stopped me midway through a beat and told me to get out of my head. You are thinking about the dancing part too much instead of just feeling the music and letting it guide you. At first I was a little confused, but as I regressed to being in my head again, I could now see how when I was thinking about the dance steps I was, in fact, dancing very rigidly. And then a beautiful thing happened. I closed my eyes for a second and listened deeply to the music and danced. All the steps that I already knew just came to me, and there was a release of joy as I leaned into the music to dance and not focus on the steps that I was taught. I had always known the steps but was missing the most important part of dancing, the *relationship* with the music.

Our lives are truly connected in so many different ways, and I hope that through the stories and anecdotes I have shared sprinkled in with small doses of research, you see the opportunity to use these five simple yet very profound principles and respective practices to deeply connect with your students but, more importantly, that you truly dance to the song of connection. Every educator has the opportunity to use their special position to connect, support, and guide children and families, especially the most vulnerable and marginalized, through the road map of success—the American Dream. Educators have the road map to the "hidden curriculum" of the American Dream—education.

My deepest hope for this book is that it will motivate, inspire, and encourage you to use these five principles to deeply connect with children and families in your school and community. At the time of writing this, we are almost at the two-year mark of undergoing a global pandemic, an exodus of teachers leaving the field of education, and the continuation of inequities dramatically and disproportionately affecting our most *marginalized* groups of students. If ever we needed to tap into our humanity, it is now. As I reflect on my life successes, they are because of educators who reached into their humanity and connected with me beyond the labels placed on me, educated me, loved me, and uplifted me in a way that encouraged me to become all that I could be. This girl, who lived in an apartment next to two large commercial trash cans in one of Austin's most impoverished neighborhoods, ate food purchased with food stamps, and was raised by a single mother who immigrated to this country and spoke little English, graduated from one of the world's most renowned universities and became a CEO because of educators like you. The five principles are not just theories, they are, in effect, the formula of my own personal success and legacy.

While my lived experience in K–12 schools was decades ago, the five principles I shared with you are very much still relevant today. If you embrace and adopt each one of the principles, you will have the opportunity to transform your practice as an educator. Educators go beyond teaching curriculum; they truly support students to reach their fullest potential.

Reviewing the Contents: A Comprehensive Recap

When educators and students connect on a human level, it can lead to building trust, enhancing motivation and engagement, providing culturally relevant instruction, supporting social-emotional development, and serving as positive role models. The connections educators make with students can contribute to a positive and inclusive educational environment that promotes effective teaching and meaningful learning experiences that go way beyond the classroom. When educators and students connect on a human level, several positive outcomes can occur. Next are just a few that were highlighted during the book.

It was a pleasure to write this book. My hope is to reignite the flame within educators like you and remind you of the principles you have always known deep in your hearts. May this book serve as a reflective tool, accompanying you throughout the school year, and occasionally nudging you to remember the incredible role you play in the lives of children—you are the guiding lights on a transformative journey, impactors of generations, members of the profession that creates all other professions. You are educators.

The introduction sets the stage, unveiling the profound position educators hold in society. With the research of Urie Bronfenbrenner's ecological systems theory as our guide, we explore the immense impact educators have on the lives of children and families. We recognize the power they possess to level the playing field and become fierce advocates, ensuring every student in their classroom receives a quality education, especially those facing the daunting challenges of poverty. It becomes apparent that our education system falls short in holistically supporting students in high-poverty communities and the dedicated educators working tirelessly in those very communities.

From there, we embarked on a journey of self-discovery and empowerment through the principles that underpin effective teaching and learning. Principle 1: Know Your Why, unveiled the extraordinary potential that lies in genuine human connections between educators and students. As trust and rapport blossom, you are encouraged to foster an environment of support and safety, encouraging students to express themselves, ask questions, and fearlessly embrace their learning journey.

Principle 2: Understand Context Beyond Compliance, inspired educators to see students as unique individuals with their own perspectives and experiences. By valuing their stories and honoring their backgrounds, we seek to ignite a fire within them, fueling their motivation and engagement in the learning process. This chapter was a reminder to become architects of inspiration, fostering a sense of belonging and empowerment regardless of what labels are placed on students.

Building upon these foundations, Principle 3: Foster Meaningful Relationships, allowed us to uncover the impact that building meaningful relationships has to the learning environment. By forging genuine connections, we gain profound insights into our students' strengths, needs, and interests. With this understanding, we learned that we can craft instruction that is not only culturally relevant but deeply impactful.

In Principle 4: Design High-Quality Learning Environments, we recognized that education extends beyond academic achievement. It becomes a catalyst for social-emotional development, with educators serving as beacons of guidance and support. By connecting on a human level, we cultivate emotional well-being, foster empathy, nurture communication skills, and ignite the flame of conflict resolution. Holistic development becomes the cornerstone of education, with educators embracing their pivotal role as cultivators of character.

Principle 5: Partner With Key Stakeholders, unveils the power of collaboration and the profound impact educators have as role models. Through meaningful connections with students, we exemplify values such as respect, compassion, and inclusivity, shaping the very fabric of their character. As we partner with parents, communities, and fellow educators, we unleash a force of change that transcends the boundaries of the classroom, enriching lives in unimaginable ways.

Finally, in "Chapter 6: Oxygen Masks Are Not Just for Airplanes," we confront the urgent reality that our education system is in a state of emergency. It calls for educators to prioritize their own well-being, acknowledging that only when they are fueled by self-care can they effectively support their students. By embracing their own self-care, educators empower themselves to be unwavering champions of change, standing on the frontlines of education's transformative journey.

Together, let us embrace these principles with a renewed sense of purpose and passion. Let us kindle the flame within ourselves and our students, shaping a future where every student's potential is realized, where education becomes a beacon of hope and empowerment. You are not just an educator—you are a catalyst for change, a source of inspiration, and a guardian of dreams. Embrace the power that lies within you and, together, let us illuminate the path to a brighter tomorrow.

In closing, let us know the profound impact educators have in shaping lives and communities. It prompts us to reflect on the transformative potential that lies within our classrooms and schools. By forging genuine connections, we have the ability to break the cycle of generational poverty and create a ripple effect of positive change. The COVID-19 pandemic has taught us the importance of reimagining how we connect with one another, and as educators, we hold the key to unlocking a future where every student thrives. Let us embrace the responsibility and privilege that comes with our role, knowing that our dedication and compassion have the power to make a lasting difference in the lives of our students and the world they will inherit. Together, through the power of human connection, we can create a brighter and more just tomorrow.

Note

1   https://www.oxfordreference.com/display/10.1093/
    acref/9780191843730.001.0001/q-oro-ed5-00007046;jsessionid=8
    D9C7B65C62A34AF44160A9272522EBE

References

Bronfenbrenner, U. (1979). *The Ecology of Human Development*. Harvard University Press.

Community-Based Transportation and Outdoor Mobility for Older Adults: A Literature Synthesis and Case Study—Scientific Figure on ResearchGate. Available from: www.researchgate.net/figure/Social-Ecological-System-Model-Urie-Bronfenbrenner-1979_fig1_335797760 [accessed 29 May, 2023]

Freire, P. (2017). *Pedagogy of the Oppressed*. Penguin Classics.

Geo-neutrinos and Earth's Interior—Scientific Figure on ResearchGate. Available from: www.researchgate.net/figure/A-sketch-of-the-Earths-interior_fig10_1756780 [accessed 29 May, 2023]

Gittell, J. H. (2016). *Transforming Relationships for High Performance: The Power of Relational Coordination*. Stanford Business Books. Available from: https://www.amazon.com/Transforming-Relationships-High-Performance-Coordination/dp/0804787018

Gonzalez, N., Moll, L. C., & Amanti, C. (Eds.). (2005). *Funds of Knowledge*. Routledge Member of the Taylor and Francis Group.

Harper, K. B. (2023, January 10). Texas budget: Lawmakers have $188.2 billion in state money. *The Texas Tribune*. Available from: www.texastribune.org/2023/01/09/texas-budget-revenue-estimate/

Know Your Why | Michael Jr. (n.d.). Available from: https://youtu.be/1ytFB8TrkTo [accessed August 8, 2021]

Lightfoot, S. L. (2016, September 28). *The Ecology of Education: Culture, Communities, and Change in Schools*, personal communication.

Mapp, K. L., & Kuttner, P. J. (2013). *Partners in Education: A Dual Capacity-Building Framework for Family-School Partnerships*. SEDL.

Mcleod, S., PhD. (2023). Bronfenbrenner's ecological systems theory. *Simply Psychology*. Available from: www.simplypsychology.org/bronfenbrenner.html

National Center for Education Statistics. (2023). Concentration of public school students eligible for free or reduced-price lunch. In *Condition of Education. U.S. Department of Education*. Institute of

Education Sciences. Available from: https://nces.ed.gov/programs/coe/indicator/clb

Schein, E. H. (2013). *Humble Inquiry: The Gentle Art of Asking Instead of Telling*. Berrett-Koehler Publishers.

Sinek, S. (2009). *Start with Why: How Great Leaders Inspire Everyone to Take Action*. Penguin Group.

Stanford Human Design, Designing for Social Systems. Available from: https://dschool.stanford.edu/programs/designing-for-social-systems

Structure of the Earth. (2023, March 8). *A Level Geography*. Available from: www.alevelgeography.com/structure-of-the-earth/

TED Talk. (2013). *Rita Pierson: Every Kid Needs a Champion* [video]. Available from: www.ted.com/talks/rita_pierson_every_kid_needs_a_champion/transcript?language=en [accessed January 6, 2023]

The Mental Models Global Laboratory. (n.d.). *What Are Mental Models?*. Available from: www.modeltheory.org/about/what-are-mental-models/

World Bank Open Data. (n.d.). *World Bank Open Data*. Available from: https://data.worldbank.org/indicator/NY.GDP.MKTP.CD?locations=FI

World Economic Forum. (2022, November 15). 10 reasons why Finland's education system is the best in the world. *World Economic Forum*. Available from: www.weforum.org/agenda/2018/09/10-reasons-why-finlands-education-system-is-the-best-in-the-world

Printed in the United States
by Baker & Taylor Publisher Services